FRENCH

GRAMMAR

THE KEY TO READING

FRENCH
GRAMMAR
THE KEY TO READING

COLETTE BRICHANT

University of California, Los Angeles

PRENTICE-HALL, INC., Englewood Cliffs, New Jersey

Prentice-Hall International, Inc., *London*
Prentice-Hall of Australia, Pty. Ltd., *Sydney*
Prentice-Hall of Canada, Ltd., *Toronto*
Prentice-Hall of India Private Ltd., *New Delhi*
Prentice-Hall of Japan, Inc., *Tokyo*

Library of Congress Catalog Card No.: 68-15847

Current printing (last digit)

10 9 8 7 6

Printed in the United States of America

PREFACE

This book is designed for use by the student whose primary objective is to acquire a reading knowledge of French. It has been carefully organized to offer a course of rapid study, and thus no unessential material is presented.

If you are a beginner, follow the lessons in the order in which they appear. Read the examples of each new grammatical point with utmost attention. Practice reading them until you can understand them without referring to the translation, for they contain both basic vocabulary and fundamental grammatical structures that must be remembered. We have tried to simplify matters by giving diagrams and tables of the more complex aspects of grammar and syntax.

In the course of the book, we gradually introduce the most important irregular verbs. You cannot be expected to memorize them all, but it is vital that you be able to recognize their most common forms. (You *must*, however, know the complete conjugations of the auxiliary verbs: **être:** *to be;* **avoir:** *to have;* **aller:** *to go.*) When you study a conjugation, regular or irregular, learn each form with its corresponding subject pronoun (e.g., **je suis, tu es, il est**); this will help you to avoid any possible confusion. Since dictionaries list only verbal infinitives, you should find Appendix E ("Stems of Irregular Verbs") to be particularly helpful.

Three readings volumes have been prepared to be used in close conjunction with *French Grammar: The Key to Reading.* The vocabulary and reading selections in each have been chosen to accommodate the needs of students in the three basic disciplines. The books are: *French for the Humanities, French for the Sciences,* and *French for the Social Sciences* (all Prentice-Hall, 1968). The first half of each volume consists of sentences for translation. They are divided into groups based on material dealt with in the chapters of the grammar (beginning immediately with Chapter I) and are cross-referenced to it. Thus they offer not only graded reading material, but also additional examples of the various grammatical points and a basic vocabulary essential to the reading of French.

By the time you reach Chapter VIII, start reading a few simple selections written by modern authors, Read a few lines at a time; after you have understood a paragraph, read it over and, if possible, go back to it a few days later. Remember that the acquisition of a new language, whatever method you may use, depends upon regular practice. Cramming before an exam can only cause confusion.

After you have studied Chapter XIII, you should be ready to begin translating literary and scholarly French, with the help of a dictionary. In the second half of the readers, you will find selections which will help you reach that stage. The texts are unsimplified; however, to facilitate the transition, we have added footnotes and cross references to the major grammatical difficulties. In the appendixes at the end of the book, we have endeavoured to present handy tables of reference. It is our hope that they will help you in your first independent ventures into French. Et je vous souhaite bon voyage . . .

C. B.

CONTENTS

CHAPTER XIV   (cont'd)

FRENCH

GRAMMAR

THE KEY TO READING

⯐ INTRODUCTION ⯑

A. THE SOUNDS OF FRENCH

Even if your immediate goal is to be able only to translate French, you will still need a general knowledge of French sounds. In the following list you will find the main elements of spelling and their respective pronunciation. The sounds are transcribed with the symbols of the International Phonetic Association. We have listed the vowels, the nasal vowels, and the important groups of vowels. We have also included the consonants that require special attention, leaving out those that have approximately the same sound in French and in English.

SPELLING	PRONUNCIATION	EXAMPLES
i	[i]	livre *book;* signe *sign;* silence *silence*
î [1]	[i]	île *island*
y	[i]	système *system;* syllabe *syllable;* hymne *hymn*
e	[ə] [2]	petit *small;* appartement *apartment;* fenêtre *window*
é [3]	[e]	théorie *theory;* téléphone *telephone;* résumé *summary*
è [4]	[ɛ]	père *father;* mère *mother;* frère *brother*
ê	[ɛ]	fête *feast;* forêt *forest*
a	[a]	table *table;* capitale *capital;* tarif *tariff*
à	[a]	à *at, to*
â	[ɑ]	âge *age;* château *castle*
o	[ɔ]	porte *door* sorte *sort, kind;* soldat *soldier*
ô	[o]	rôle *role, part;* hôtel *hotel;* hôpital *hospital*

---

[1] This accent [^] is called a circumflex accent (see below).
[2] This sound is often called the "mute" or "fleeting" *e* because in many cases it is either slurred or not pronounced at all.
[3] This accent [′] is called an acute accent.
[4] This accent [`] is called a grave accent.

1

SPELLING (CONT'D.)	PRONUNCIATION (CONT'D.)	EXAMPLES (CONT'D.)
u	[y]	musique *music;* nature *nature;* surface *surface*
û	[y]	sûr *sure*
ai	[ɛ]	air *air;* maître *master;* clair *clear*
eu	[ø]	deux *two;* feu *fire*
œ	[œ]	sœur *sister;* cœur *heart*
au	[o]	mauvais *bad;* saut *jump*
eau	[o]	eau *water;* beauté *beauty;* chapeau *hat*
ou	[u]	rouge *red;* amour *love;* journal *newspaper*
oi	[wɑ]	roi *king;* joie *joy;* trois *three*
an	[ɑ̃] [5]	blanc *white;* banque *bank;* franc *frank, franc*
en	[ɑ̃] [5]	prudent *prudent;* silence *silence;* vent *wind*
on	[ɔ̃] [5]	bon *good;* nation *nation;* fondation *foundation*
in, ain, ein	[ɛ̃] [5]	vin *wine;* pain *bread;* serein *serene*
un	[œ̃] [5]	un *a, one*
ch	[ʃ]	cheval *horse;* cheminée *chimney;* chimie *chemistry*
gn	[ɲ]	magnifique *wonderful;* dignité *dignity*
ph	[f]	physique *physics;* pharmacie *pharmacy*
j	[ʒ]	journal *newspaper;* jour *day;* janvier *January*
c+a	[ka] [6]	café *coffee;* calme *calm*
c+o	[kɔ] [6]	collection *collection*
c+on	[kɔ̃] [6]	conférence *lecture;* contre *against*
c+u	[ky] [6]	particule *particle;* ridicule *ridiculous*
c+e	[sə] [6]	force *strength;* farce *farce*
c+i	[si] [6]	cité *city;* cinéma *cinema*
ç+a	[sa] [6]	ça *that*
ç+o	[swa] [6]	François *Francis*
ç+on	[sɔ̃] [6]	garçon *boy;* leçon *lesson*
ç+u	[sy] [6]	reçu *receipt*
g+a	[ga] [7]	galerie *gallery;* garde *guard*
g+o	[gɔ] [7]	gorge *throat, gorge*
g+u	[gi] [7]	guide *guide*
g+e	[ʒə] [7]	âge *age;* sage *wise*
g+i	[ʒi] [7]	agitation *agitation;* girafe *giraffe*
h	(no sound)	homme *man;* habitude *habit*

---

[5] These sounds [ɑ̃, ɔ̃, ɛ̃ and œ̃] are the nasal vowels. When they are pronounced, the air goes simultaneously through the mouth and through the nose. The four nasal vowels can be grouped in a short, simple phrase: **un bon vin blanc** *a good white wine.*

[6] The letter *c* has a hard sound [k] when it is followed by *a, o,* or *u.* It has a soft sound [s] when it is followed by *e* or *i.* A cedilla [ş] is placed under the *c* when the *c* must have a soft sound, even though it is followed by *a, o,* or *u.* Later on, you will see that the pronunciation of the *c* determines orthographical changes in certain verbs (see §6.7).

[7] The letter *g* has a hard sound [g] when it is followed by *a, o,* or *u.* It has a soft sound [ʒ] when it is followed by *e* or *i.* Later on, you will see that the pronunciation of the *g* determines orthographical changes in certain verbs (see §6.7).

B. INTRODUCTION TO READING

Many French and English words stem from a common Greek or Latin origin. The first aim of a student who wishes to acquire a reading knowledge of French should be to take full advantage of his knowledge of English. Words that are identical in both languages or that have a common root are called cognates.

COGNATES

auto	camp	long	style
aviation	hôtel	mode	surprise
boulevard	idiot	port	village

-able

acceptable	appréciable	navigable	stable
admirable	formidable	remarquable	vénérable

-al

animal	général	légal	normal
capital	immoral	moral	vital

-ible

admissible	convertible	flexible	perceptible
compréhensible	extensible	fusible	visible

-tion

accusation	animation	élection	nation
admiration	combustion	émotion	radiation

DISSIMILAR ENDINGS

Although many cognates have common endings, many others do not.

-é → -y

beauté	férocité	intensité	stabilité
célébrité	identité	objectivité	vanité

-eur → -or

accélérateur	directeur	générateur	modérateur
administrateur	docteur	inspecteur	professeur

-ie → -y

anatomie	énergie	industrie	philosophie
astronomie	géographie	métallurgie	photographie

-ique → -ic, -ical

alphabétique	cylindrique	énergétique	magique
analytique	cynique	historique	mathématique
atomique	électrique	logique	physiologique

-isme → -ism

absolutisme	communisme	naturalisme	réalisme
capitalisme	dualisme	paganisme	socialisme

-ment, -ement[8] → -ly, -ally

calmement	électriquement	généralement
commercialement	fermement	légalement

The Circumflex Accent

It is often possible to find the translation of a word that contains a circumflex accent [^] by adding an *s* after the vowel that has this accent:

[^] → s

fête	*feast*	**île**	*isle, island*
forêt	*forest*	**maître**	*master*
hâte	*haste*	**mât**	*mast*
hôte	*host*	**plâtre**	*plaster*
hôpital	*hospital*	**vêtement**	*(vestment)[9] clothing*

---

[8] This ending is characteristic of adverbs derived from adjectives.
[9] Quite often a very common French word is similar to a less common English word.

French Words Used
in Modern English

Many French words have been adopted in modern English, though their original meaning has often been altered.

FRENCH WORD	BASIC MEANING
à propos	*concerning*
au revoir[10]	*good-by*
bon voyage	*good journey*
bureau	*desk, office*
carte blanche[11]	*white card*
coup	*blow*
crême de menthe	*cream of mint*
cuisine	*kitchen, cooking*
ensemble	*group, whole, together*
genre	*gender, kind, type*
nom de plume	*pen name*
par avion	*by plane*
petit	*small*
plateau	*tray, plateau*
raison d'état	*reason of state*
raison d'être	*reason for being*
rapport	*relationship, relation*
répondez s'il vous plaît	*answer (if you) please*
soirée	*evening*
suite	*sequence, following*

Among the numerous American cities with French names are:

NAME OF CITY	LITERAL MEANING
Baton Rouge	*red stick*
Des Moines	*of the monks*
Detroit	*strait* (geog.)
Eau Claire	*clear water*
Fond du Lac	*bottom of the lake*
La Grange	*the barn*
Montclair	*clear mountain*
Terre Haute	*high land*

---

[10] **Cf. voir:** *to see.*
[11] Note that in French the adjective usually follows the noun.

⊫ CHAPTER I ⊐

A. DEFINITE ARTICLES

§1.1   French nouns are either masculine or feminine. When you study a noun, learn it with its definite article.[1] The definite article reflects the gender and number of the noun that it modifies.

§1.2   FORMS

	SINGULAR		PLURAL	
M.	le livre	*the book*	les livres	*the books*
F.	la porte	*the door*	les portes	*the doors*

§1.3 **NOTE**

1. When a noun begins with a vowel or with a vowel sound,[2] **le** and **la** become **l'**. This eliminates the presence of two vowel sounds in a row, which would not be harmonious in spoken French. The forms become:

	SINGULAR		PLURAL	
M.	l'autobus	*the bus*	les autobus	*the buses*
F.	l'université	*the university*	les universités	*the universities*

---

[1] No general rule can indicate the gender of nouns. Certain endings characterize masculine nouns, others feminine nouns (see §2.8); sometimes the meaning of the word can indicate its gender (**le soldat:** *soldier*, **la femme:** *woman*), but these cases are not numerous. Students who are seeking only a reading knowledge of French need not remember the gender of all the nouns they study.

[2] The letter *h* is never pronounced. In most cases it has no effect on the pronunciation.

2. When **les** precedes a noun that begins with a vowel or with a vowel sound, the *s*, which is normally mute, becomes voiced and is sounded *z*. This sounding of a final consonant that normally is mute is called a "link."

| les arbres | *the trees* | les idées | *the ideas* |
| les hommes | *the men* | les habitudes | *the habits* |

§1.4   MEANINGS

The French definite article has two basic and radically different meanings:

1. **It indicates a definite person or thing.** In this case, it plays the same role as its English counterpart; it pin-points one particular thing or person.

Le livre de l'étudiant.	*The book of the student.*[3]
La porte de la classe.	*The door of the classroom.*
Le dictionnaire est[4] sur la table.	*The dictionary is on the table.*

In these sentences we have referred to one particular book, a particular classroom, etc.

| **Les dictionnaires sont sur la table.** | *The dictionaries are on the table.* |

In this sentence we have referred to one particular group of dictionaries.

2. **It indicates an entire category.** In this case it has no counterpart in English. The article indicates that the noun stands for an entire category or a general concept.

La musique est un art.	*Music is an art.*
Le fer est un métal.	*Iron is a metal.*
La patience est une vertu.	*Patience is a virtue.*
Les hommes sont mortels.	*Men are mortal.*

La musique, le fer, la patience, les hommes are used in an absolute sense.

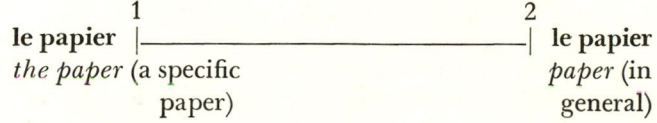

	1		2	
le papier				**le papier**
the paper (a specific paper)				*paper* (in general)

| **Le papier est sur la table.** | *The paper is on the table.* |
| **Le papier est combustible.** | *Paper is combustible.* |

---

[3] This sentence could also be translated: *the student's book.* Note that French has no true possessive case.

[4] For the verb **être:** *to be,* see §1.6.

§1.5   3. The definite article is also used in the following cases:

(a) *Before geographical names* (other than names of cities):[5]

la France	l'Amérique	le Canada
les Etats-Unis	la Seine	le Mississippi

✗ (b) *Before titles* (military, academic, etc.), <u>except when addressing a</u> <u>person directly</u>:

le général de Gaulle	*General de Gaulle*
le docteur Brun	*Doctor Brun*
le professeur Dupont	*Professor Dupont*
l'oncle Paul	*Uncle Paul*
Bonjour, docteur Brun.	*Good morning, Doctor Brun.*
Au revoir, général de Gaulle.	*Good-by, General de Gaulle.*

(c) *Before names of languages,* except when they are used with the verb **parler:** *to speak:*

Le français[6] est facile.	*French is easy.*
Je parle français.	*I speak French.*

The use of the definite article is also highly idiomatic and should be studied more thoroughly after you have acquired a somewhat greater knowledge of the language.

B. ÊTRE AND AVOIR

§1.6   In order to read simple sentences, one must learn the present tense of the two most important verbs: **être:** *to be* and **avoir:** *to have.* These verbs are irregular and should be studied with the utmost care.

INFINITIVE	**être** *to be*	**avoir** *to have*
1 P. SG.	**je suis** *I am*	**j'ai** *I have*
2 P. SG.	**tu es** *you are, thou art*	**tu as** *you have*
3 P. SG. M.	**il est** *he/it is*	**il a** *he/it has*
—— F.	**elle est** *she/it is*	**elle a** *she/it has*
1 P. PL.	**nous sommes** *we are*	**nous avons** *we have*
2 P. PL.	**vous êtes** *you are*	**vous avez** *you have*
3 P. PL. M.	**ils sont** *they are*	**ils ont** *they have*
—— F.	**elles sont** *they are*	**elles ont** *they have*

---

[5] Geographical terms will be studied more thoroughly in §§14.2 and 14.4.

[6] Note that the French do not capitalize the names of languages or nationalities (when used adjectively). [Cf. **le français:** French (language); **français, -e:** French. *But* **le Français, la Française:** the Frenchman, the French woman.

1. **Je** is not capitalized unless it begins a sentence. It becomes **j'** when the following word begins with a vowel (cf. §1.2).

2. The **tu** form is usually familiar; it is used to address children, relatives, close friends, and pets. It is seldom found in literary French except in certain religious or poetical writings to indicate respect.

3. French has no neuter subject pronoun. Since all nouns are either masculine or feminine, things are referred to as **il** or **elle**, according to their gender. Bear this in mind when translating.

Il est petit.	*He is small (the man, the child, etc.).*
Il est petit.	*It is small (the tree, the boat, etc.).*

§1.8

C. IL Y A

Il y a, perhaps the most common expression in French, attests to the existence of one or more persons or things. It is invariable and should be translated as *there is* or *there are.* **Il y a** must not be confused with **il a:** *he/it has.*

Il y a un livre sur la table.	*There is a book on the table.*
Il y a dix étudiants dans la classe.	*There are ten students in the class(room).*

Compare the use of **il y a** with that of **être:**

Il y a un livre sur la table; il est bleu.	*There is a book on the table; it is blue.*
Il y a un étudiant dans la classe; il est grand.	*There is a student in the class-(room); he is tall.*

☞ CHAPTER II ☜

A. INDEFINITE ARTICLES

Indefinite articles refer to objects or persons not specifically identified.

§2.1   Forms

	SINGULAR		PLURAL	
M.	**un livre**	*a book*	**des livres**	*books*
F.	**une maison**	*a house*	**des maisons**	*houses*

§2.2   Meanings and Translations

1. The indefinite articles **un** and **une** should generally be translated by $a(n)$.

> **un livre**   *a book* (any book; cf. **le livre:** *the book*)
> **un homme**   *a man*
> **une femme** *a woman*

2. **Un** and **une** are also the masculine and feminine forms of the numeral *one*. Normally the context indicates whether to translate by *a* or by *one*.

§2.3   3. **Des,** the plural indefinite article, has no specific counterpart in English. Sometimes it may be translated as *some*. However, remember that **des** indicates an indefinite number of items (*not* a limited number) and that therefore, in most cases, it should not be translated.

J'ai des livres.	*I have books.*
Il a des amis.	*He has friends.*
Il y a des kangourous en Australie.	*There are kangaroos in Australia.*

NOTE

Des (the indefinite article) should not be confused with the contraction of the preposition **de** (*of, from*) and the definite article **les.** When **des** is a contracted article, it usually means *of the, from the.* (See §4.5.)

B. FEMININE AND PLURAL
OF ADJECTIVES AND NOUNS

In French, adjectives agree in gender and number with the noun they modify.

§2.4   FEMININE OF ADJECTIVES

Normally the feminine is formed by adding an *e* to the masculine form.

un livre intéressant	*an interesting book*
une étude intéressante	*an interesting study*
un livre vert	*a green book*
une porte verte	*a green door*

The feminine of special groups of adjectives will be studied in §2.6.

§2.5   PLURAL OF ADJECTIVES

The plural is usually formed by adding an *s* to the singular; this *s* is mute.

un livre intéressant	*an interesting book*
des[1] livres intéressants	*interesting books*
une découverte importante	*an important discovery*
des découvertes importantes	*important discoveries*

---

[1] See §2.3.

In the feminine plural the adjective takes *es*. The plural of special groups of adjectives will be studied in §2.10.

§2.6

FEMININE OF
SPECIAL GROUPS OF ADJECTIVES

MASCULINE ENDING	FEMININE ENDING	EXAMPLE
-e	(no change)	jeune *young*
-er	-ère	premier/première *first*
-el	-elle	naturel/naturelle *natural*
-en	-enne	ancien/ancienne *ancient, former*
-et	-ette	net/nette *neat, clean*
-eil	-eille	pareil/pareille *alike, similar*
-eur	-euse	flatteur/flatteuse *flattering*
-eux	-euse	heureux/heureuse *happy*
✷ -as	-asse	bas/basse *low*
✷ -ais	-aisse	épais/épaisse *thick*
-on	-onne	bon/bonne *good*
-os	-osse	gros/grosse *big, fat*
-ot	-otte	sot/sotte *silly*
-ul	-ulle	nul/nulle *worthless, void*
-f	-ve	actif/active *active* bref/brève *brief*
-c	{ -che *or* -que	blanc/blanche *white* public/publique *public*

§2.7

ADJECTIVES IRREGULAR
IN THE FEMININE

MASCULINE	FEMININE	TRANSLATION
doux	douce	*soft, gentle*
faux	fausse	*false, wrong*
frais	fraîche	*fresh, cool*
gentil	gentille	*nice, kind*
grec	grecque	*Greek*
jaloux	jalouse	*jealous*
long	longue	*long*

Three adjectives have three forms: masculine, feminine (irregular), and a special form that is used when it precedes a masculine noun beginning with a vowel sound (cf. §1.3).

MASCULINE	SPECIAL MASCULINE FORM	FEMININE	TRANSLATION
beau	bel	belle	*beautiful*
nouveau	nouvel	nouvelle	*new*
vieux	vieil	vieille	*old*

Le livre est beau.	*The book is beautiful.*
Le bel arbre.	*The beautiful tree.*
L'homme est vieux.	*The man is old.*
Un vieil homme.	*An old man.*
Le livre est nouveau.	*The book is new.*
Le nouvel ambassadeur.	*The new ambassador.*

§2.8 FEMININE FORMS OF NOUNS

A few nouns have both a masculine and a feminine form. There are three possibilities:

1. The two forms are alike; only their gender differs:

l'artiste	l'artiste	*artist*
le secrétaire	la secrétaire	*secretary*

2. An *e* is added to form the feminine noun:

l'ami	l'amie	*friend*
le boulanger	la boulangère	*baker*
le bourgeois	la bourgeoise	*middle-class person*
le marchand	la marchande	*merchant*

3. A special ending characterizes the feminine noun:

le directeur	la directrice	*director*
l'éducateur	l'éducatrice	*educator*
le chanteur	la chanteuse	*singer*
le danseur	la danseuse	*dancer*
le comte	la comtesse	*count, countess*
le duc	la duchesse	*duke, duchess*

§2.9 PLURAL OF NOUNS

The plural of nouns is usually formed by adding an *s* to the singular. This *s* is mute.

	SINGULAR		PLURAL
le livre	*the book*	les livres	*(the) books*
une université	*a university*	des universités	*universities*
un homme célèbre	*a famous man*	des hommes célèbres	*famous men*

§2.10   PLURAL OF SPECIAL GROUPS OF NOUNS AND ADJECTIVES

For the plural of certain categories of nouns and adjectives, see Table 2.1.

TABLE 2.1

ENDINGS	NOUNS	ADJECTIVES (MASC. FORM)
-s -x -z → no change	le cas/les cas *case* le prix/les prix *price, prize* le gaz/les gaz *gas*	gros/gros *big* heureux/heureux *happy, fortunate* ————
-au → -aux -eau → -eaux	le tuyau/les tuyaux *pipe* le bateau/les bateaux *boat*	———— beau/beaux *beautiful, handsome*
-al → -aux	le journal/les journaux *newspaper*	général/généraux *general*
-eu → -eux (*n.*) -eus (*adj.*)	le feu/les feux *fire*	bleu/bleus *blue*

§2.11   NOUNS IRREGULAR IN THE PLURAL

1. Eight nouns in **-ail** change to **-aux.** The most common are:

le corail	les coraux	*coral*
l'émail	les émaux	*enamel*
le travail	les travaux	*work*
le vitrail	les vitraux	*stained glass*

2. Seven nouns in **-ou** add an **x.** The most common are:

le bijou	les bijoux	*jewel*
le caillou	les cailloux	*pebble*
le genou	les genoux	*knee*

3. The following are completely irregular:

l'aïeul	les aïeux	*ancestor*
le ciel	les cieux[2]	*sky, Heaven*
l'œil	les yeux	*eye*

§2.12

C. POSITION OF ADJECTIVES

In French, as in English, adjectives can qualify a noun through a verb: **la maison est blanche:** *the house is white.* This case presents no difficulty. They can also qualify the noun directly: **une maison blanche:** *a white house.* In this case they usually follow the noun. In English the word order is almost invariably the opposite.

une découverte importante	*an important discovery*
une table ronde	*a round table*
une industrie importante et prospère	*an important and prosperous industry*

However, about ten short and very common adjectives normally precede the noun that they modify:

bon	*good*	un bon livre	*a good book*
mauvais	*bad*	un mauvais livre	*a bad book*
jeune	*young*	un jeune chien	*a young dog*
vieux	*old*	un vieux château	*an old castle*
grand	*large*	une grande maison	*a large house*
petit	*small*	une petite auto	*a small car*
long	*long*	un long voyage	*a long trip*
gros	*big*	un gros dictionnaire	*a big dictionary*
beau	*beautiful*	un beau tableau	*a beautiful painting*
joli	*pretty*	une jolie femme	*a pretty woman*

Numbers and the adjectives **autre:** *other* and **dernier:** *last* precede the noun.

un autre livre	*another book*
trois livres	*three books*
le troisième jour	*the third day*

NOTE

The position of adjectives can be influenced by the rhythm of the sentence or by the intention of the author. Transpositions for stylistic effect are often found in literary French.

---

[2] In painting, however, the plural is **les ciels.** For example: **les ciels de Turner:** *the skies of Turner.*

D. DEMONSTRATIVE ADJECTIVES

Demonstrative adjectives point out specific items. They precede the noun and agree with it in gender and number.

	SINGULAR		PLURAL	
M.	ce livre	*this book*	ces livres	*these books*
F.	cette porte	*this door*	ces portes	*these doors*

NOTE

When the masculine demonstrative adjective precedes a word beginning with a vowel (or vowel sound), **ce** becomes **cet** to make the pronunciation more harmonious.[3]

cet animal   *this animal*   cet auteur   *this author*

In the plural, the *s* of **ces** is pronounced *z* when it precedes a vowel sound:

ces éléments   *these elements*

E. POSSESSIVE ADJECTIVES

§2.14   Possessive adjectives indicate ownership. Their forms are determined both by the person of the possessor and by the gender and number of the thing possessed.

M. SG.	mon livre	*my book*
F. SG.	ma maison	*my house*
M. PL.	mes livres	*my books*

§2.15   FORMS

For a convenient list of the various forms, see Table 2.2.

---

[3] Cf. §2.7.

TABLE 2.2

Possessive Adjectives

GENDER AND NUMBER OF THINGS POSSESSED

PERSON OF THE POSSESSOR	MASCULINE SINGULAR	FEMININE SINGULAR	MASCULINE & FEMININE PLURAL	ENGLISH EQUIVALENT
1 P. SG.	mon livre	ma[4] maison	mes livres, maisons	*my*
2 P. SG.	ton —	ta —	tes —	*your*
3 P. SG. M.	son —	sa —	ses —	*his, her, its*
3 P. SG. F.	son —	sa —	ses —	*his, her, its*
1 P. PL.	notre —	notre —	nos —	*our*
2 P. PL.	votre —	votre —	vos —	*your*
3 P. PL. M. & F.	leur —	leur —	leurs —	*their*

§2.16   TRANSLATION

The translation of possessive adjectives presents no difficulties except in the case of **son, sa,** and **ses.** Remember that in French, possessive adjectives agree in gender and number with the thing possessed; in English, they agree with the possessor (his, her, its).

L'homme a son livre, sa plume et ses papiers.	*The man has his book, his pen, and his papers.*
Ma sœur a son livre, sa plume et ses papiers.	*My sister has her book, her pen, and her papers.*
Le chien a son lait, sa viande et ses biscuits.	*The dog has its milk, its meat, and its biscuits.*

---

[4] Before feminine nouns that begin with a vowel or vowel sound, the possessive adjectives **ma, ta,** and **sa** are replaced by **mon, ton,** and **son** to make the pronunciation more harmonious: **mon amie:** *my (girl) friend;* **son idée:** *his, her idea.*

F. COMPARATIVES

In French, as in English, there are three comparatives: equality, superiority, and inferiority.

§2.17   EQUALITY

$$\boxed{\text{aussi} + \left\{ \begin{array}{c} \text{adj.} \\ \text{or} \\ \text{adv.} \end{array} \right\} + \text{que}} \rightarrow as + \left\{ \begin{array}{c} \text{adj.} \\ \text{or} \\ \text{adv.} \end{array} \right\} + as$$

La poste est aussi grande que l'é-
cole.

The post office is as large as the
school.

Cet élève lit[5] aussi rapidement que
les autres.

This student reads as rapidly as the
others.

§2.18   SUPERIORITY

French has one single form.

$$\boxed{\text{plus} + \left\{ \begin{array}{c} \text{adj.} \\ \text{or} \\ \text{adv.} \end{array} \right\} + \text{que}} \rightarrow \left\{ \begin{array}{l} more + \left\{ \begin{array}{c} \text{adj.} \\ \text{or} \\ \text{adv.} \end{array} \right\} + than \\ \text{-}er + than \end{array} \right.$$

L'Amérique est plus grande que
l'Europe.

America is larger than Europe.

Le professeur lit plus rapidement
que l'élève.

The teacher reads faster than the
student.

§2.19   INFERIORITY

$$\boxed{\text{moins} + \left\{ \begin{array}{c} \text{adj.} \\ \text{or} \\ \text{adv.} \end{array} \right\} + \text{que}} \rightarrow less + \left\{ \begin{array}{c} \text{adj.} \\ \text{or} \\ \text{adv.} \end{array} \right\} + than$$

Cette expérience est moins intéres-
sante que l'autre.

This experiment is less interesting
than the other.

---

[5] From lire: to read.

1. <u>When equality is shown in a negative sentence</u> (see §7.1), **si often** replaces **aussi.**

> **Paul n'est pas si (aussi) intelligent que son frère.**   *Paul is not as intelligent as his brother.*

2. With *a number* the forms are:

$$\left. \begin{array}{l} \textbf{plus de } + \text{ number} \\ \textbf{moins de } + \text{ number} \end{array} \right\} \rightarrow \begin{array}{l} \textit{more than (or over)} + \text{ number} \\ \textit{less than} + \text{ number} \end{array}$$

> **Il y a plus de dix étudiants dans la classe.**   *There are more than ten students in the class.*

3. When *two amounts* are compared, the forms are:

$$\left. \begin{array}{l} \textbf{autant de} \\ \textbf{plus (davantage) de} \\ \textbf{moins de} \end{array} \right\} + \text{noun} + \textbf{que} \rightarrow \left\{ \begin{array}{l} \textit{as much} \\ \textit{more} \\ \textit{less} \end{array} \right. + \text{noun} + \left\{ \begin{array}{l} \textit{as} \\ \textit{than} \\ \textit{than} \end{array} \right.$$

> **J'ai autant de travail que le professeur.**   *I have as much work as the teacher.*

4. When *two actions* are compared, the forms are:

$$\text{verb} + \left\{ \begin{array}{l} \textbf{autant} \\ \textbf{plus (davantage)} \\ \textbf{moins} \end{array} \right\} + \textbf{que} \rightarrow \text{verb} + \left\{ \begin{array}{l} \textit{as much as} \\ \textit{more than} \\ \textit{less than} \end{array} \right.$$

> **J'étudie autant que Pierre.**   *I study as much as Peter.*

5. Note, too, the constructions **de plus en plus:** *more and more;* **de moins en moins:** *less and less;* **plus** + verb . . . **plus** + verb: *the more . . . the more;* **moins** + verb . . . **moins** + verb: *the less . . . the less.*

> **Je travaille de plus en plus.**   *I study more and more.*
> **Je comprends de moins en moins.**   *I understand less and less.*
> **Plus je travaille, plus je suis fatigué.**   *The more I work, the more tired I am.*

G.   SUPERLATIVES

There are two kinds of superlatives: superiority and inferiority. They are always preceded by a definite article or a possessive adjective. They are found before or after the noun they qualify (see §2.12).

$$\left.\begin{array}{c} \text{def. article} \\ \text{or} \\ \text{poss. adj.} \end{array}\right\} + \text{plus} + \left\{\begin{array}{c} \text{adj.} \\ \text{or} \\ \text{adv.} \end{array}\right. \rightarrow \left\{\begin{array}{l} \textit{the most} \\ \textit{-est} \end{array}\right. + \text{adj. or adv.}$$

Paris est la ville la plus importante en France.	*Paris is the most important city in France.*
Il a son plus vieux costume.	*He has (is wearing) his oldest suit on.*
Il travaille le plus vite de tous.	*He works the fastest of all.*

$$\left.\begin{array}{c} \text{def. article} \\ \text{or} \\ \text{poss. adj.} \end{array}\right\} + \text{moins} + \left\{\begin{array}{c} \text{adj.} \\ \text{or} \\ \text{adv.} \end{array}\right. \rightarrow \textit{the least} + \text{adj. or adv.}$$

Ce livre est le moins intéressant de la collection.	*This book is the least interesting in the collection.*

One adjective (**bon:** *good*) and one adverb (**bien:** *well*) are irregular in the comparative and superlative of superiority. All other forms are regular.

	ADJECTIVE	ADVERB
POSITIVE	**bon** *good*	**bien** *well*
COMPARATIVE	**meilleur que** *better than*	**mieux que** *better than*
SUPERLATIVE	**le meilleur** *the best*	**le mieux** *the best*

Since **meilleur** is an adjective, it agrees:

Le vin est meilleur que l'eau.	*Wine is better than water.*
La Sorbonne est la meilleure école.	*The Sorbonne is the best school.*
Paul travaille mieux que Pierre.	*Paul works better than Peter.*
Le malade va[6] mieux.	*The patient is* (lit., *goes*) *better.*

---

[6] From **aller:** *to go.* See §3.8. **Aller** has many meanings. One of the most common is *to feel;* for example: **Comment allez-vous?** *How are you?*

NOTE

The forms **pire que:** *worse than* and **le pire:** *the worst* are often found in abstract sentences. Otherwise the adjective **mauvais:** *bad* is regular.

Ce café est plus mauvais que l'autre.	*This coffee is worse than the other.*
Ce remède est pire que le mal.	*This remedy is worse than the evil.*

The regular superlative **le plus petit** means the smallest in size. The irregular form **le moindre** means *the least, the most insignificant.*

J'ai la plus petite maison.	*I have the smallest house.*
Le professeur remarque la moindre faute.	*The teacher notices the least mistake.*

§2.24   IRREGULAR VERBS IN THE PRESENT

Study the following irregular verbs:[7]

FAIRE *to make, to do*

je fais	nous faisons
tu fais	vous faites
il (elle) fait	ils (elles) font

Common noun form: **le fait** *fact*

Verbs conjugated like **faire:**
défaire[8] *to undo*
refaire[9] *to do over, to repeat*

LIRE *to read*

je lis	nous lisons
tu lis	vous lisez
il (elle) lit	ils (elles) lisent

Like **lire:**
relire *to read over*

PRENDRE *to take*

je prends	nous prenons
tu prends	vous prenez
il (elle) prend	ils (elles) prennent

Like **prendre:**
apprendre *to learn*
comprendre *to understand, to comprehend, to include*
entreprendre *to undertake*
reprendre *to take again*
surprendre *to surprise*

---

[7] We shall introduce a certain number of irregular verbs in each chapter. They should be studied with extreme care, as they are among the most common verbs in the language.

[8] The prefix *de-* always indicates a negative idea. Cf. English *dis-* or *un-*.

[9] The prefix *re-* always indicates a repetition.

🏳 CHAPTER III 🏴

§3.1 ## A. THE INFINITIVE

French verbs fall into three groups, which can be identified by the infinitive ending. The infinitive is not preceded by any specific word, such as *to* in English.

GROUP	VERB STEM	+	INFINITIVE ENDING	→	INFINITIVE	
first [1]	march-		er		**marcher**	*to walk*
second	fin-		ir		**finir**	*to finish*
third	vend-		re		**vendre**	*to sell*
	part-		ir		**partir**	*to leave*
	recev-		oir		**recevoir**	*to receive*

NOTE

The third group consists of a few verbs that present many irregularities. It is important to distinguish between the verbs of the second group (all of which have an infinitive in **-ir**) and a certain number of verbs of the third group that have an infinitive in **-ir.** Their conjugations are different.

---

[1] More than nine French verbs out of ten belong to the first group. They are all regular except **aller:** *to go* (see §3.8).

B. THE PRESENT TENSE

§3.2   The present tense is formed by adding the following endings to the stem:

FIRST GROUP		SECOND GROUP[2]		THIRD GROUP	
marcher		finir		vendre	
je march	e	je fin	is	je vend	s
tu march	es	tu fin	is	tu vend	s
il march	e	il fin	it	il vend	—
nous march	ons	nous fin	issons	nous vend	ons
vous march	ez	vous fin	issez	vous vend	ez
ils march	ent	ils fin	issent	ils vend	ent[3]

MEANINGS AND TRANSLATIONS

Basic meanings

§3.3   1. *Contemporary actions or situations.*

L'étudiant est dans la classe.   *The student is in the class(room).*

NOTE

French has no progressive form (i.e., auxiliary *to be* plus present participle). Consequently, the French present tense can be translated by an English present tense or by a progressive form, depending on the context:

Il étudie en ce moment.   *He is studying right now.*
Il étudie beaucoup.   *He studies a lot.*

French has no emphatic verb form. Consequently, **il étudie** can also be translated as *he does study,* depending on the context.

---

[2] All verbs in the second group follow the same pattern of conjugation.
[3] As you progress in the study of French conjugations, you will notice certain patterns:
    (*a*) The endings of the second person singular always end with an *s* (except in the imperative; see §3.13).
    (*b*) An ending in **-ons** always denotes a first   person plural.
    (*c*) "   "   " **-ez**   "   "   " second   "   "
    (*d*) "   "   " **-ent**   "   "   " third   "   "

2. *Usual or constant actions or situations.*

Les hommes sont mortels.	*Men are mortal.*
Le cuivre est un métal.	*Copper is a metal.*
Paul étudie chaque jour.	*Paul studies every day.*

3. *Actions or situations that began in the past and have continued until the present moment.* Usually the French sentence is constructed with **depuis:** *since.* This word comes from **de:** *from* + **puis:** *then.*

Il est à Paris depuis le premier janvier 1967.	*He has been in Paris since the first of January 1967.*

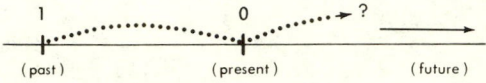

The action began in the past (1) and has gone on until the present moment (0). To express this idea English uses a past tense, but French uses a present tense because the action is still going on.

Il travaille depuis deux heures.	*He has been working for two hours.*
Nous sommes dans la classe depuis une heure.	*We have been in the class(room) for an hour.*

NOTE

To express duration, French uses **pendant:** *for, during.* In a sentence with **pendant,** the tense of the verb indicates the time of the action.[4]

Chaque jour il lit pendant une heure.	*Every day he reads for an hour.*

Other meanings

The present tense is sometimes used to express an action that took place very recently or that is expected to take place in the near future.

Il arrive de Paris.	*He is just back from Paris.*
Je viens dans une minute.	*I'm coming in a minute.*

In literary French, the present tense is sometimes used to express past actions. In the course of an account written in the past, an author may suddenly shift to the present tense in order to give more vividness to an important event. This "historic present" (*présent historique*) should normally be translated by a past tense in English.

---

[4] For other expressions of time, see Chap. IX.

Aller: *to go* is the only irregular verb of the first group. **Venir:** *to come* belongs to the third group. Both are highly irregular and must be studied with the utmost attention.

ALLER *to go*	VENIR *to come*
je vais *I go (am going)*	je viens *I come (am coming)*
tu vas	tu viens
il va	il vient
nous allons	nous venons
vous allez	vous venez
ils vont	ils viennent

§3.9   A basic expression is formed with each of these verbs.

> **aller** in the present + inf. → near future ✱

Je vais lire ce livre.	*I am going to read this book.*
Elle va écrire la lettre.	*She is going to write the letter.*
Nous allons travailler.	*We are going to work.*

> **venir** in the present + **de** + inf. → recent past ✱

Il vient de finir.	*He has just finished.*
Je viens de lire le journal.	*I have just read the paper.*
Je viens de voir Paul.	*I have just seen Paul.*

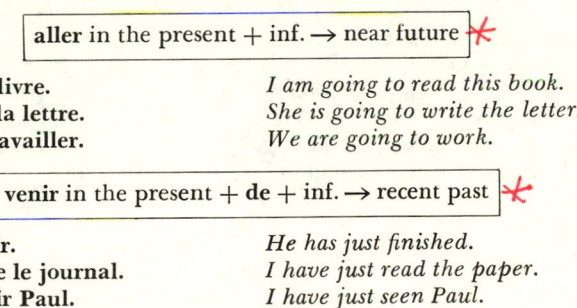

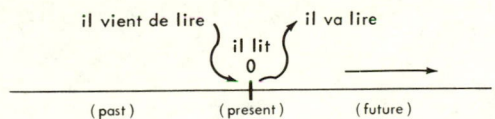

§3.10

C. THE PAST PARTICIPLE

The past participle is used to form all compound tenses. It is also frequently used as an adjective.

GROUP	INFINITIVE	ENDING OF PAST PARTICIPLE	PAST PARTICIPLE
first	marcher	é	marché *walked*
second	finir	i	fini *finished*
third	vendre	u *(certain verbs only)*	vendu *sold*

NOTE

All verbs of the first and second groups have regular past participles. Some verbs of the third group form their past participle with the ending **-u**, others with **-i**, **-is**, or **-ert** (see §3.17).

INFINITIVE	PAST PARTICIPLE	INFINITIVE	PAST PARTICIPLE
lire *to read*	**lu**	prendre *to take*	**pris**
mettre *to put*	**mis**	rendre *to give back*	**rendu**

Usually all verbs derived from an irregular verb follow the same pattern of conjugation. For example:

INFINITIVE		PAST PARTICIPLE
prendre	*to take*	**pris**
apprendre	*to learn*	**appris**
comprendre	*to understand*	**compris**
entreprendre	*to undertake*	**entrepris**
reprendre	*to take again*	**repris**
surprendre	*to surprise*	**surpris**

D. THE PASSÉ COMPOSÉ

§3.11   The passé composé[5] is a compound tense. It is formed with the present tense of an auxiliary (**avoir** or **être**) and the past participle. Most verbs are conjugated with **avoir**.[6]

FIRST GROUP	SECOND GROUP	THIRD GROUP
j'ai marché *I (have) walked*	**j'ai fini** *I (have) finished*	**j'ai vendu** *I (have) sold*
tu as marché	**tu as fini**	**tu as vendu**
il a marché	**il a fini**	**il a vendu**
nous avons marché	**nous avons fini**	**nous avons vendu**
vous avez marché	**vous avez fini**	**vous avez vendu**
ils ont marché	**ils ont fini**	**ils ont vendu**

---

[5] It is advisable to use this term so as to avoid possible confusion with other French past tenses.

[6] For verbs conjugated with **être**, see Chap. VIII.

Verbs in the passé composé express completed actions, either of the remote or of the recent past. They may be translated by the English present perfect or past, depending on context.

J'ai lu ce livre.	*I read (have read) this book.*
Il a acheté une maison l'année der-nière.	*He bought a house last year.*
Pasteur a fait beaucoup d'expé-riences.[7]	*Pasteur made many experiments.*

E.   THE IMPERATIVE

§3.13   The imperative, used to give orders or to express wishes or warnings, has no subject.

The French imperative has three persons:

	FIRST GROUP		SECOND GROUP		THIRD GROUP	
2 P. SG.	march	e	fin	is	vend	s
1 P. PL.	march	ons	fin	issons	vend	ons
2 P. PL.	march	ez	fin	issez	vend	ez

§3.14   TRANSLATION

The translation of the second person singular and plural presents no difficulties, provided you do not confuse it with the present tense. Remember: The imperative has no subject.

Regarde!	*Look!*
Entrez et fermez la porte.	*Come in and close the door.*

For the first person plural the English equivalent is *let us.*

Commençons.	*Let's begin.*
Partons.	*Let's go.*
Etudions[8] ce problème.	*Let's study this problem.*

---

[7] Depending on context, l'**expérience** (*f.*) means either *experiment* or *experience.*

[8] Note that the acute, grave, and circumflex accents are usually not used on capital letters. The cedilla, however, is always used.

F. VOICI, VOILÀ

Voici: *here is, here are* and **voilà:** *there is, there are*[9] are used to point out objects, persons, or abstract ideas. They may be followed by either a singular or plural noun. Usually **voici** refers to objects that are close to the person speaking and **voilà** to those that are further away.

Voici un livre.	*Here is a book.*
Voici les lettres.	*Here are the letters.*
Voilà la porte.	*There is the door.*

IRREGULAR PRESENTS
AND PAST PARTICIPLES

METTRE *to put*		TENIR *to hold*	
je mets	nous mettons	je tiens	nous tenons
tu mets	vous mettez	tu tiens	vous tenez
il met	ils mettent	il tient	ils tiennent

Past participle: **mis** (*irregular*)
Passé composé: **j'ai mis**
Verbs conjugated like **mettre:**
admettre *to admit*
commettre *to commit*
omettre *to omit*
remettre *to put back, to remit*
soumettre *to submit*

Past participle: **tenu** (*regular*)
Passé composé: **j'ai tenu**
Like **tenir:**
appartenir *to belong*
contenir *to contain*
détenir *to detain*
maintenir *to maintain*
retenir *to retain*
soutenir *to sustain*

IRREGULAR PAST PARTICIPLES

Study the following irregular past participles:[10]

---

[9] **Voici** comes from **voir:** *to see* + **ici:** *here;* **voilà,** from **voir** + **là:** *there.*
[10] Beginners should study the irregular past participles within an example, preferably with the first person singular of the passé composé.

INFINITIVE	PAST PARTICIPLE	PASSÉ COMPOSÉ
prendre[11] *to take*	pris	j'ai pris
ouvrir *to open*	ouvert	j'ai ouvert
couvrir *to cover*	couvert	j'ai couvert
découvrir *to discover*	découvert	j'ai découvert
recouvrir *to cover again*	recouvert	j'ai recouvert
rouvrir *to reopen*	rouvert	j'ai rouvert
offrir *to offer*	offert	j'ai offert
souffrir *to suffer*	souffert	j'ai souffert
lire *to read*	lu	j'ai lu
relire *to read over*	relu	j'ai relu
voir *to see*	vu	j'ai vu
revoir *to see again, to check*	revu	j'ai revu
faire *to make, to do*	fait	j'ai fait
défaire *to undo*	défait	j'ai défait
refaire *to do over*	refait	j'ai refait

---

[11] For verbs conjugated like **prendre**, see §3.10.

🏳 CHAPTER IV 🏴

A. PREPOSITIONS À AND DE

§4.1   French has two key prepositions: <u>à</u> (*at, in, to*)[1] and <u>de</u> (*from, of, about*). Both have several shades of meaning and are found in many idiomatic expressions. When translating, one should always consider both the meaning of the verb and the general context.

§4.2   ### CONTRACTIONS

When **à** and **de** precede **le** or **les,** they contract:

à + le → ⬚ au ⬚	de + le → ⬚ du ⬚
à la *no contraction*	de la *no contraction*
à l' " "	de l' " "
à + les → ⬚ aux ⬚	de + les → ⬚ des ⬚

§4.3   ### MEANINGS AND TRANSLATIONS
OF <u>A</u>

1. *Location*. Usual translation: *at, in*.

Il est au jardin.	*He is in the garden.*
Elle travaille à la maison.	*She works at home.*
Il étudie à l'université.	*He studies at the university.*

---

[1] The preposition à must not be confused with the third person singular of the verb **avoir.** (See §1.6.)

2. *A specific moment.* Usual translation: *at.*

au commencement	*at the beginning*	à minuit	*at midnight*
à la fin	*at the end*	à huit heures[3]	*at eight o'clock*
à midi[2]	*at noon*	à Noël	*at Christmastime*

3. *A direction* when used with a verb of motion. Usual translation: *to.*

Il va au jardin.	*He goes to the garden.*
Ce train va à Paris.	*This train goes to Paris.*

4. *Destination.* When something is passed by one person to another, the recipient is preceded by à. Usual translation: *to.*[4]

Il parle au garçon.	*He speaks to the boy.*
J'écris à mon ami.	*I write to my friend.*
Je donne un livre à mon frère.	*I give a book to my brother.*

5. *Possession,* when used with the verbs **être:** *to be* and **appartenir:** *to belong.*[5]

Ce livre est à Paul.	*This book is Paul's.*
Cette auto appartient au docteur.	*This car belongs to the doctor.*

6. The *purpose* or *nature* of that which precedes. Such expressions can seldom be translated literally. One should analyze each element carefully before translating.

une machine à écrire	*a typewriter*
une machine à calculer	*a calculating machine*
une salle à manger	*a dining room*
une tasse à thé	*a teacup*
une maison à vendre	*a house for sale*
le travail à faire	*the work to be done*
une lettre à signer	*a letter to be signed*
facile à faire	*easy to do*

7. The *characteristic* of the verb or noun that precedes.

un bébé aux yeux bleus	*a blue-eyed baby*
un courant à haute fréquence	*a high-frequency current*
un animal à sang chaud	*a warm-blooded animal*

---

[2] The prefix **mi-**, found in many words, indicates the middle. Cf. English *mid-*.

[3] Lit., *at eight hours;* **une heure:** *an hour.*

[4] The use of prepositions is not parallel in both languages; in many cases the French preposition à has no equivalent in English. For example: **Il téléphone à son ami.** *He telephones his friend.*

[5] See §3.16.

MEANINGS AND TRANSLATIONS
OF D̲E̲

1. *Origin or beginning.* Usual translation: *from.*

Cet avion vient de New York.	*This plane comes from New York.*
Ce train va de Paris à Lyon.	*This train goes from Paris to Lyon.*
Le musée est ouvert de midi à quatre heures.	*The museum is open from noon until four o'clock.*

2. *The cause of an action.* Often translated by: *of, from.*

Il est mort de faim.	*He died of hunger.*
Elle récite de mémoire.	*She recites from memory.*
Il procède d'une façon empirique.	*He proceeds in an empirical way.*

3. *The topic or subject matter.* Usual translation: *about.*

Le professeur parle de la Première Guerre mondiale.	*The teacher talks about the First World War.*
Ce livre traite de l'éducation des enfants arriérés.	*This book deals with the education of retarded children.*

4. *Noun + de + noun.* In this construction, the second noun determines the first one.[6] It usually indicates:

(*a*) the material or substance:

une maison de bois	*a wooden house*
une statue de bronze	*a bronze statue*
une feuille de papier	*a sheet of paper*
une classe de chimie	*a chemistry course*
un livre de référence	*a reference book*
une tasse de thé	*a cup of tea*[7]
un chef d'Etat	*a head of state*

(*b*) the purpose or characteristic:

une histoire[8] d'amour	*a love story*
une auto de course	*a race car*
un travail de précision	*a work of precision*
la clé de la maison	*the key to the house*
le résultat de l'expérience	*the result of the experiment*

(*c*) the possessor:

la maison de mon ami[9]	*my friend's house*

---

[6] As a rule, the words that determine follow the words that are determined. Cf. §2.12.

[7] Cf. **une tasse à thé**: *a teacup* and **une tasse de thé**: *a cup of tea;* **un verre à vin**: *a wine glass* and **un verre de vin**: *a glass of wine.*

[8] Depending on context, **l'histoire** (*f.*) means either *history* or *story.*

[9] This construction is very common because French does not have a true possessive case.

le livre du professeur	*the professor's book*
le travail des enfants	*the children's work*

5. *The partitive.* See below.

B. THE PARTITIVE

§4.6   The partitive is expressed by the preposition **de,** and is usually followed by the definite article. (For exceptions, see §4.8.)

§4.7   Meanings and Translations

As we have seen (§1.4), the definite article can express: (1) a *definite* person or thing or (2) a *general* category.

Le vin de ce restaurant est bon.	*This restaurant's wine is good.*
Le vin contient de l'alcool.	*Wine contains alcohol.*

The partitive, on the other hand, expresses an *indefinite* amount or an *indefinite* number of items.

Pierre boit du vin.	*Peter drinks (is drinking) wine.*

In affirmative sentences, *some* may sometimes render the meaning of the French; in most cases, however, no word should be used in English:[10]

Je mange de la viande chaque jour.	*I eat meat every day.*
Les enfants boivent du lait.	*Children drink milk.*
Le Brésil produit du café.	*Brazil produces coffee.*
Elle fait des fautes.	*She makes mistakes.*
Il y a des bâtiments modernes à Paris.	*There are modern buildings in Paris.*

In negative[11] or interrogative[12] sentences, the partitive can usually be translated by *any* or *no.*

---

[10] Normally, *some* indicates a *limited* amount, while the French partitive indicates an *indefinite* amount, large or small.

[11] See Chap. VII.

[12] See §§4.11-4.14.

| Y a-t-il des manuscrits à la Biblio-
thèque Nationale? | *Are there any manuscripts at the
National Library?* |

Normally, the partitive **de** is followed by a definite article (see §4.7). However, in three cases, it is not.

1. *After a negation.*

| **Je ne mange pas de viande.** | *I don't eat any meat.* |
| **Il n'y a pas de volcans en France.** | *There are no volcanoes in France.* |

2. *After an expression of quantity.*[13]

| **Pierre boit beaucoup de vin.** | *Peter drinks a lot of wine.* |

3. *Before a plural noun preceded by an adjective.*[14]

| **A Paris il y a de vieilles maisons.** | *In Paris there are old houses.* |
| **Il a acheté de belles roses.** | *He bought beautiful roses.* |

NOTE

The preceding paragraphs show that **de** can have several meanings. Don't forget that you must always first consider the meaning of the verb, and then translate **de** within the general context.

Il vient de la gare.	*He is coming from the station.*
Il vient des Antilles.	*He comes from the West Indies.*
Il mange de la viande.	*He eats meat.*
Il parle de la musique moderne.	*He is talking about modern music.*
Il a des amis.	*He has friends.*
Il mange des gâteaux.	*He eats (is eating) cakes.*
Il étudie la civilisation des Mayas.	*He is studying the Mayan civilization (the civilization of the Mayas).*

C. EXPRESSIONS OF QUANTITY

§4.9   Expressions of quantity are used with things that can be divided into units and counted (e.g., books, houses, pens, etc.) or with substances that

[13] See §4.10.
[14] See §2.12.

TABLE 4.1

Main Expressions of Quantity

Expressions used with things that can be divided and counted	*Expressions used with substances or abstract ideas that cannot be divided*
IN EXCLAMATIVE AND INTERROGATIVE SENTENCES	**IN EXCLAMATIVE AND INTERROGATIVE SENTENCES**
Que de livres! *So many books!*	Que de travail! *So much work!*
Combien de livres! *So many books!*	Tant de travail! *So much work!* — abstract
Combien de livres?[15] *How many books?*	Combien de travail? *How much work?*
PRONOMINAL AND ADVERBIAL EXPRESSIONS	**PRONOMINAL AND ADVERBIAL EXPRESSIONS**
trop de livres *too many books*	trop de travail *too much work*
énormément de livres *a great number of books*	énormément de travail *a considerable amount of work*
tellement de livres *so many books*	tellement de travail *so much work*
tant de livres *so many books*	tant de travail *so much work*
plus de[16] livres *more books*	plus de[16] travail *more work*
la plupart[17] des livres *most of the books*	la plupart[17] du travail *most of the work*
beaucoup de livres *many books*	beaucoup de travail *a lot of work*
passablement de livres *quite a few books*	passablement de travail *quite a bit of work*
bien des livres *lots of books* (often fam.)	bien du travail *a lot of work* (often fam.)

[15] Cf. §4.12.
[16] See §2.20.
[17] Note the use of the definite article.

la plupart des livres
bien des livres

TABLE 4.1—Continued

PRONOMINAL AND ADVERBIAL EXPRESSIONS

pas mal de livres *lots of books* (fam.)
autant de livres *as many books*
assez de livres *enough books*
plusieurs livres *several books*
quelques livres *a few books*
peu de[18] **livres** *few books*
guère de livres *hardly any books*
moins de livres *fewer books*

No de

NOUNS

une masse de livres *a mass of books*
un millier de[19] **livres** *about a thousand books*
des milliers de livres *thousands of books*
une centaine[19] **de livres** *about a hundred books*
des centaines de livres *hundreds of books*
une douzaine de livres *a dozen books*
une dizaine de livres *about ten books*
une série de livres *a series of books*
une collection de livres *a collection of books*

PRONOMINAL AND ADVERBIAL EXPRESSIONS

pas mal de travail *quite a bit of work* (fam.)
autant de travail *as much work*
assez de travail *enough work*
peu de[18] **café** *little coffee*
un peu de[18] **café** *a little coffee, a small amount of coffee*
guère de café *hardly any coffee*
moins de café *less coffee*

NOUNS

une masse de pierres *a mass of stones*
une goutte d'eau *a drop of water*
une tonne de charbon *a ton of coal*
un kilo de pain *a kilo of bread*
une livre[20] **de pain** *a pound of bread*
une tasse de café *a cup of coffee*
une bouteille de vin *a bottle of wine*
une poignée de sel *a handful of salt*

[18] **Peu de:** *few, little* must not be confused with **un peu de:** *a little.* **Peu** can also be followed by an adjective or a participle: **ce livre est peu intéressant:** *this book is not very interesting;* **cette montagne est peu élevée:** *this mountain is not very high.*
[19] **Mille:** *one thousand;* **cent:** *one hundred.*
[20] Do not confuse **la livre:** *pound* with **le livre:** *book.*

cannot be divided (e.g., liquids, abstract concepts, etc.). Some of the expressions are common to both categories, others can be used with only one of them.

Most expressions of quantity end with the preposition **de,** followed by the noun (with no definite article).

§4.10   The most common expressions of quantity are found in Table 4.1.

D. INTERROGATIVE SENTENCES

§4.11   An interrogative sentence always ends with a question mark—a clue not to be overlooked. In most interrogative sentences, the subject follows the verb, but this is not an absolute criterion. No auxiliary, such as *do* or *is,* is used in French.

§4.12   INTERROGATIVE WORDS
                         AND CONSTRUCTIONS

Qui . . . ? Qui est-ce qui . . . ? [21] *Who . . . ?*

Qui frappe à la porte?	*Who is knocking on the door?*
Qui a fini?	*Who has finished?*
Qui est-ce qui désire une tasse de café?	*Who wants a cup of coffee?*

Qui . . . ? Qui est-ce que . . . ? Whom . . . ?

Qui aime-t-elle? [22]	*Whom does she love?*
Qui est-ce que vous avez vu?	*Whom have you seen?*

Qu'est-ce qui . . . ? What . . . ?

Qu'est-ce qui tombe?	*What is falling?*
Qu'est-ce qui arrive? [23]	*What is happening?*

---

[21] The long forms are found mostly in conversational French. See the general table of interrogative pronouns, §4.15.

[22] In the inverted interrogative constructions, a *t* is inserted between the verb forms that end with a vowel sound and the pronouns **il(s)** and **elle(s)** in order to make the pronunciation smoother.

[23] Depending on context, **arriver** can mean either *to arrive* or *to happen.*

Que . . . ? Qu'est-ce que . . . ? *What . . . ?*

Que font les enfants?	*What are the children doing?*
Qu'a dit le Président?	*What has the President said?*
Qu'est-ce qu'il fait?	*What is he doing?*

Preposition + qui . . . ? *Preposition + whom, whose.*

A qui est ce livre?	*Whose book is this?*
De qui parlez-vous?	*Of whom are you speaking?*
Avec qui travaille-t-il?	*With whom does he work?*

Preposition + quoi . . . ? *Preposition + what . . . ?*

A quoi pensez-vous?	*What are you thinking about?*
Avec quoi font-ils cette liqueur?	*With what do they make this liquor?*
Pourquoi[24] avez-vous accepté?	*Why have you accepted?*

Quel, Quelle, Quels, Quelles[25] + noun . . . ? *What, which + noun . . . ?*

Quel livre lisez-vous?	*Which book are you reading?*
Quelle heure est-il?	*What time is it?*
Quelle est la réponse?	*What is the answer?*

Lequel, Laquelle, Lesquels, Lesquelles . . . ? *Which one . . . ?*

When **lequel** is preceded by **à** or **de**, it contracts (cf. §4.2): **auquel, auxquels, auxquelles** and **duquel, duquels, duquelles**. There is of course no contraction in the feminine singular.

Voici deux livres. Lequel préférez-vous?	*Here are two books. Which one do you prefer?*
Il y a trois théâtres dans cette ville. Auquel désirez-vous aller?	*There are three theatres in this city. To which one do you wish to go?*

Où . . . ? [26] *Where . . . ?*

Où va ce train?	*Where is this train going?*
D'où venez-vous?	*Where do you come from?*

Combien . . . ? *How much, how many . . . ?*

Combien coûte ce livre?	*How much does this book cost?*
Combien produit cette usine?	*How much does this factory produce?*

---

[24] Note that **pourquoi** (*lit.*, for what) is written as one word.
[25] Note that **quel** is an adjective and therefore agrees with the noun.
[26] Do not confuse **où:** *where* with **ou:** *or* (no accent).

Comment . . . ? How . . . ?

> **Comment allez-vous?** [27] — *How are you?*
> **Comment les Egyptiens ont-ils construit les pyramides?** — *How did the Egyptians build the pyramids?*

§4.13   STRUCTURE OF INTERROGATIVE SENTENCES

1. *If the subject is a pronoun,* it follows the verb. When the verb is in a compound tense, the subject pronoun comes directly after the auxiliary.

> **Est-il au bureau?** — *Is he in the office?*
> **A qui écrivez-vous?** — *To whom are you writing?*
> **Va-t-elle à l'école?** — *Does she go to school?*
> **Y a-t-il une université à Paris?** — *Is there a university in Paris?*
> **Avez-vous compris la leçon?** — *Have you understood the lesson?*

2. *If the subject is a noun,* a double subject is used. The regular subject precedes the verb, then is repeated after the verb in the form of the corresponding subject pronoun:

> **Le directeur est-il au bureau?** — *Is the director in the office?*
> **Le mercure est-il un métal?** — *Is mercury a metal?*

When the verb is in a compound tense, the subject pronoun comes after the auxiliary:

> **Marie a-t-elle téléphoné?** — *Has Marie telephoned?*
> **Les délégués ont-ils vu la lettre?** — *Have the delegates seen the letter?*

Generally the subject is not repeated when the sentence begins with an interrogative word:

> **Où va ce train?** (or: **Où ce train va-t-il?**) — *Where does this train go?*

§4.14   EST-CE QUE . . . ?
N'EST-CE PAS . . . ?

Est-ce que is used mostly in conversational French. It is never followed by an inversion.

---

[27] See Chap. II, note 6.

TABLE 4.2

MAIN INTERROGATIVE PRONOUNS

	PERSONS	THINGS
SUBJECT	**Qui, qui est-ce qui** *Who* **Qui parle?** **Qui est-ce qui parle?** } *Who is talking?*	**Qu'est-ce qui** *What* **Qu'est-ce qui tombe?** *What is falling?*
DIRECT OBJECT	**Qui, qui est-ce que** *Whom* **Qui voyez-vous?** **Qui est-ce que vous voyez?** } *Whom do you see?*	**Que, qu'est-ce que** *What* **Que lisez-vous?** **Qu'est-ce que vous lisez?** } *What are you reading?*
INDIRECT OBJECT *(object of a preposition)*	**Prep. + qui** Prep. + *whom, whose* **Avec qui travaille-t-elle?** } *With whom does* **Avec qui est-ce qu'elle travaille?** } *she work?*	**Prep. + quoi** Prep. + *what* **Avec quoi écrit-il?** } *With what is he writing?* **Avec quoi est-ce qu'il écrit?** }

Est-ce qu'il a fini?	*Has he finished?*
Est-ce que le travail est fini?	*Is the work finished?*

N'est-ce pas is used mostly in conversational French; it is invariable. It is used to ask for confirmation of the preceding statement.

Il est au bureau, n'est-ce pas?	*He is in the office, isn't he?*
Elle a envoyé la lettre, n'est-ce pas?	*She sent the letter, didn't she?*
Il n'est pas malade, n'est-ce pas?	*He isn't sick, is he?*

§4.15 For a convenient table of the main interrogative pronouns, see Table 4.2.

§4.16

IRREGULAR PRESENTS
AND PAST PARTICIPLES

BOIRE *to drink*

je bois	nous buvons
tu bois	vous buvez
il boit	ils boivent

Past participle: **bu**
Passé composé: **j'ai bu**

ÉCRIRE *to write*

j'écris	nous écrivons
tu écris	vous écrivez
il écrit	ils écrivent

Past participle: **écrit**
Passé composé: **j'ai écrit**

PRODUIRE *to produce*

je produis	nous produisons
tu produis	vous produisez
il produit	ils produisent

Past participle: **produit**
Passé composé: **j'ai produit**
Common noun form:
   le produit *product, yield*
Verbs conjugated like **produire:**
conduire *to drive, to lead,*
   to conduct
construire *to build, to construct*
déduire *to deduce, to deduct*
détruire *to destroy*
instruire *to instruct, to teach*
réduire *to reduce*

ᛚᛚ CHAPTER V ᛚᛚ

PRONOUNS

§5.1   A pronoun is a word used in the place of a noun. Thus far we have used only the subject pronouns:

je	*I*		nous	*we*
tu	*you, thou*		vous	*you*
il	*he, it*		ils	*they*
elle	*she, it*		elles	*they*

§5.2   ON

On is another subject pronoun (cf. Latin: *homo;* German: *man;* English: *one*), and is always used with a verb in the third person singular. It indicates that the action is done by one or several agents who are not specifically named. It can be translated by *we, you, they, one, someone, people,* or by a passive construction, depending on context.

A Mexico[1] on parle espagnol.	*In Mexico City people speak Spanish (Spanish is spoken).*
On a construit une nouvelle université.	*A new university has been built (They built . . .).*
On dit que ce livre est intéressant.	*People say that this book is interesting.*
On trouve beaucoup d'illustrations dans le dictionnaire Larousse.	*There are many illustrations in the Larousse dictionary (Many illustrations are found . . .).*

---

[1] **Mexico:** *Mexico City;* le **Mexique:** Mexico.

In French, as in English, a direct object denotes the person or thing acted upon; it answers the question *whom?* or *what?* In **il voit le livre:** *he sees the book,* the noun (**le livre**) is the direct object of the verb (**voir**) and can be replaced by the direct object pronoun **le: il le voit:** *he sees it.*

§5.4   Direct object pronouns should be studied with a simple sentence:

il	me	voit	*he sees me*
il	te	voit	*he sees you*
il	le	voit	*he sees him, it*
il	la	voit	*he sees her, it*
il	nous	voit	*he sees us*
il	vous	voit	*he sees you*
il	les	voit	*he sees them*

§5.5 **NOTE**

1. Direct object pronouns are used for persons or things.

2. They precede the verb except when the verb is in the affirmative imperative. When the verb begins with a vowel sound, **me, te, le, la** become **m', t', l', l'** (cf. §1.3).

3. When the verb is in the affirmative imperative, the object pronoun follows, linked by a hyphen. The pronouns **me** and **te** become **moi** and **toi** to make the pronunciation easier.

Aidez-moi.   *Help me.*   **Aidez-la.**   *Help her.*

4. When the verb is in the negative imperative,[2] the object pronoun precedes:

Ne me tuez pas.   *Don't kill me.*   **Ne le dites pas.**   *Don't say it.*

5. The pronouns **le** and **la** should not be confused with the definite article. An article precedes a noun; an object pronoun, a verb.

6. The object pronouns **nous** and **vous** must not be confused with the subject pronouns. An object pronoun stands between the subject and the verb (except in the affirmative imperative). Besides, a verb must always agree with its subject.

Vous nous avez aidé.   *You have helped us.*
Nous vous remercions.   *We thank you.*

---

[2] Negative constructions will be studied in Chap. VII. Generally, a negation consists of: **ne** +verb + **pas.**

SPECIAL MEANINGS

OF THE OBJECT PRONOUN LE

Sometimes the object pronoun **le** stands for neither a person nor a thing; it stands for:

§5.6   1. *An adjective or a noun used predicatively.* If a man is asked: **Etes-vous malade?** *Are you sick?*, he answers: **Oui, je le suis./Non, je ne le suis pas:** *Yes, I am./No, I am not.* If a woman is asked the same question, she also answers: **Oui, je le suis./Non, je ne le suis pas.**

    Le replaces adjectives and nouns used predicatively, regardless of gender and number. Usually, in these cases, it should not be translated.

Etes-vous le capitaine? Oui, je le suis.	*Are you the captain? Yes, I am.*
Est-elle infirmière?[3] **Oui, elle l'est.**	*Is she a nurse? Yes, she is.*

§5.7   2. *An entire idea* expressed in the preceding clause.

Paul est à la bibliothèque. Oui, je le sais.	*Paul is in the library. Yes, I know (it).*
Cet homme est infirme; ne l'oubliez pas.	*This man is crippled; don't forget.*

§5.8   3. *The second part of a comparative* (in literary French). After a comparative (**plus . . . que, aussi . . . que, moins . . . que,** etc.) **le** should never be translated. Many contemporary French authors omit it.

Cet homme est plus riche que vous (le) pensez.	*This man is wealthier than you think.*

§5.9   INDIRECT OBJECT PRONOUNS

In French, indirect object pronouns stand for an object that is introduced by a preposition. We shall study: (1) the indirect object pronouns that stand for an object preceded by **à** and (2) the indirect object pronoun that stands for an object introduced by **de**.

Pronouns used to replace **à** + *object*

§5.10   1. *For things:* **y**

    Y precedes the verb (except in the affirmative imperative). Since y

---

[3] Note that the indefinite article is not used with professions in certain constructions with **être**.

stands for **à** + *noun,* it can usually be translated by: *there, to that place, at that place, about that* (see §4.3).

Il est à Paris. → **Il y est.**	*He is there.*
Il étudie à Londres. → **Il y étudie.**	*He studies there.*
Il va à l'école. → **Il y va.**	*He goes (there).*
Il répond à la question. → **Il y répond.**	*He answers it.*
Il pense à ce problème.[4] → **Il y pense.**	*He thinks about it.*

NOTE

The pronoun **y** is also used to replace nouns that are preceded by other prepositions indicating location: **en:** *in,* **dans:** *in, inside,* **sur:** *on,* **sous:** *under,* **entre:** *between,* etc.

Le livre est-il sur la table? Oui, il y est.	*Is the book on the table? Yes, it is.*

Sometimes **y** need not be translated at all. This is due to the fact that French demands a more formal grammatical structure than English.

Allez-vous à la gare? Oui, j'y vais.	*Are you going to the station? Yes, I am (going there).*
Ce mot est-il dans le dictionnaire? Oui, il y est.	*Is this word in the dictionary? Yes, it is (there).*

§5.11 2. *For persons* the following pronouns are used:

il	me	parle	*he speaks to me*
il	te	parle	*he speaks to you*
il	lui	parle	*he speaks to him*
il	lui	parle	*he speaks to her*
il	nous	parle	*he speaks to us*
il	vous	parle	*he speaks to you*
il	leur	parle	*he speaks to them*

NOTE

§5.12 1. Indirect object pronouns precede the verb except in the affirmative imperative. When the verb begins with a vowel sound, **me** and **te** become **m'** and **t'**.

2. When the verb is in the affirmative imperative, the indirect object

---

[4] **Penser:** *to think* is generally constructed with the preposition **à**. For example: **il pense à son travail:** *he thinks about his work;* **il pense à son ami:** *he thinks about his friend;* **il pense à lui:** *he thinks about him.* **Penser de** means *to think of, to have an opinion of;* for example: **qu'est-ce qu'il pense de ce livre?** *what does he think of this book?* The noun **la pensée** means *thought, thinking, philosophy.*

penser à
penser de

pronoun follows, linked by a hyphen. **Me** and **te** become **moi** and **toi** to make the pronunciation easier.

Dites-moi qui vous êtes.   *Tell me who you are.*

3. **Lui** is used for both the masculine and feminine.[5] When the identity of the object *must* be specified, a disjunctive pronoun is added (see §§5.16-5.17).

Il lui parle, à elle.   *He speaks to her.*

§5.13   4. When translating a sentence with an indirect object pronoun, one must bear in mind that the use of prepositions is not parallel in both languages. For instance, when a thing or message is passed from one person to another, the name of the recipient is always preceded by **à** (see §4.3) and thus can be replaced by an indirect object pronoun.

Je parle à mon ami. → **Je lui parle.**	*I speak to him.*
Je réponds à mon ami. → **Je lui réponds.**	*I answer him.*
Je téléphone à mon ami. → **Je lui téléphone.**	*I phone him.*
Je demande un livre à mon ami. → **Je lui demande un livre.**	*I ask him for a book.*

parler à
répondre à
téléphoner à

§5.14 *Pronoun used to replace **de** + object:* **en** *(for things only)*

En precedes the verb (except in the affirmative imperative). Since it stands for **de** + noun, its translation depends on the contextual meaning of **de** (see §§4.4, 4.7). It can often be rendered by: *from there, of that, about that, some.* Sometimes it does not correspond to any specific English word.

1. ***De*** *expresses the origin, cause, or subject matter.*

Monsieur Brun vient-il de Paris? Oui, il en vient.	*Does Mr. Brun come from Paris? Yes he does* (lit., *come from there*).
Son chien est mort hier; il en est triste.	*His dog died yesterday; it makes him sad* (lit., *he is sad about it*).

2. ***De*** *has a partitive meaning.*

A-t-il des livres? Oui, il en a.	*Does he have any books? Yes he does* (lit., *he has some of them*).
Si vous avez du café, donnez-m'en.	*If you have any coffee, give me some (of it).*

---

[5] In some rare cases, **lui** is also used to refer to things and abstract concepts.

3. *De is part of an idiomatic expression.*

J'ai besoin de[6] ce livre. → J'en ai besoin. *I need it.*

Je suis sûr[7] de cela.[8] → J'en suis sûr. *I am sure of it.*

Il est surpris de ce résultat. → Il en est surpris. *He is surprised (about it).*

§5.15 <u>NOTE</u>

<u>En</u> can be used with a number or an expression of quantity (see §4.10). In these instances it can be used to replace persons.

Avez-vous un frère? J'en ai deux. *Do you have a brother? I have two (of them).*

Connaissez-vous un médecin dans cette ville? J'en connais plusieurs. *Do you know a doctor in this city? I know several (of them).*

En is often used with impersonal expressions (see §13.17).

Il faut[9] de l'argent pour voyager; il en faut beaucoup. *You've got to have money to travel; you've got to have a lot (of it).*

There is no special pronoun to replace **de** when it occurs with the name of a person. The preposition is retained and a disjunctive pronoun used.

§5.16 DISJUNCTIVE PRONOUNS

The disjunctive pronouns are:

il parle de	moi	*he talks about me*
il parle de	toi	*he talks about you*
il parle de	lui	*he talks about him*
il parle d'	elle	*he talks about her*
il parle de	nous	*he talks about us*
il parle de	vous	*he talks about you*
il parle d'	eux	*he talks about them* (m.)
il parle d'	elles	*he talks about them* (f.)

---

[6] **Avoir besoin de:** *to need* (lit., *to have need of*). (See §7.17.)

[7] Do not confuse **sur:** *on, upon* with **sûr:** *sure.*

[8] The demonstrative **cela:** *this, that* refers to a general idea (see §11.20).

[9] **Il faut,** a very common impersonal expression, has numerous possible translations. Its basic meaning is *it is necessary,* but should be translated in context. (See §13.17).

§5.17 Disjunctive pronouns are used:

1. *After a preposition.*

Il parle avec elle.	*He speaks with her.*
Je travaille pour eux.	*I work for them.*

When used after à, the disjunctive pronoun is emphatic (see §5.12):

Il lui parle à elle, pas à moi.	*He speaks to her, not to me.*

2. *After c'est and ce sont (it is).*

C'est moi qui ai écrit cet article.	*I am the one who wrote this article (lit., it is I).*
C'est lui qui a commis le crime.	*He is the one who (has) committed the crime.*

3. *To stress a subject pronoun.*

Moi, je veux partir.	*I want to leave!*
Lui, il est coupable.	*He is guilty!*
Vous, vous faites une faute.	*You are making a mistake!*

4. *When a verb has two subjects.*

Pierre et moi, nous[10] **sommes fatigués.**	*Peter and I are tired.*
Lui et son frère sont à la maison.	*He and his brother are at home.*

5. *In the second part of a comparison.*

Il est plus fort que moi.	*He is stronger than I.*

*6. *After ne . . . que (nothing but).*[11]

Elle n'aime que lui.	*He is the only one that she likes (lit., she likes only him).*

7. *Before a relative pronoun* **qui:** *who,* **que:** *whom,* **dont:** *of whom.*[12]

Lui qui est jeune, il peut travailler.	*He is young; he can work* (or: *since he is young . . .*)

8. *As an isolated subject* in an exclamation. In this case, an auxiliary is usually added in English.

Qui a cassé le vase? Lui!	*Who broke the vase? He did.*
Qui veut un verre de vin? Moi!	*Who wants a glass of wine? I do.*

---

[10] Quite often when a verb has two subjects, they are repeated in terms of a plural subject pronoun.

* Items 6-8 are less common than the preceding uses of the disjunctive pronoun.

[11] See §§7.2-7.3.

[12] See §§7.8-7.9; 7.12.

Two object pronouns can be used together. Both precede the verb (except in the affirmative imperative). They appear in the following order:

me te nous vous	come before	le la les	come before	lui leur	come before	y	comes before	en

When translating, each pronoun should be carefully analyzed.

Il me le donne.	*He gives it to me.*
Elle le lui demande.	*She asks him (her) for it.*
Il y en a.	*There is (are) some.*
Ils nous le prêtent.	*They are lending it to us.* *prêta*

When the verb is in the affirmative imperative, the direct object pronoun precedes the indirect object pronoun (**y** and **en** *always* come last):

Donnez-le-moi.	*Give it to me*
Donnez-nous-en.	*Give us some.*
Rendez-la-lui.	*Return it to him (her).*

§5.19   For a convenient summary of the pronouns, see Table 5.1.

dans *in, inside, into*	**devant** *in front of*
en *in*	**derrière** *behind, in back of*
sur *on, upon*	**près de** *close to, near*
sous *under*	
au-dessus de *above*	**au milieu de** *in the middle of*
au-dessous de *below, beneath*	**à l'extérieur de** *outside of*
entre *between, among*	**à l'intérieur de** *inside*

TABLE 5.1

Subject and Object Pronouns

SUBJECT PRONOUNS		OBJECT PRONOUNS					DISJUNCTIVE PRONOUNS
		DIRECT OBJECT PRONOUNS (*persons and things*)	INDIRECT OBJECT PRONOUNS				
			object of preposition à		*object of preposition de*		
			THINGS	PERSONS	THINGS	PERSONS	
1 P. SG.	je	me		me			
2 P. SG.	tu	te		te			moi
3 P. SG. M.	il	le		lui			toi
3 P. SG. F.	elle	la		lui			lui
3 P. SG. IMPERS.	(on)	(se)[13]	y	—	en	de +	elle (soi)[13]
1 P. PL.	nous	nous		nous			nous
2 P. PL.	vous	vous		vous			vous
3 P. PL. M.	ils	les		leur			eux
3 P. PL. F.	elles	les		leur			elles

[13] For reflexive pronouns, see Chap. VI.

DIRE *to tell, to say*

je dis	nous disons
tu dis	vous dites[14]
il dit	ils disent

Past participle: **dit**
Passé composé: **j'ai dit**
Verbs conjugated like **dire:**
contredire *to contradict* [15]
interdire *to forbid* [15]
prédire *to predict* [15]
redire *to repeat*

[handwritten margin note: vous contredisez]

VOIR *to see*

je vois	nous voyons
tu vois	vous voyez
il voit	ils voient

Past participle: **vu**
Passé composé: **j'ai vu**
Common noun form:
　la vue *sight; view*
Like **voir:**
prévoir *to foresee*
revoir *to see again, to check*

POUVOIR *can, may,*[16]
to be able

je peux	nous pouvons
tu peux	vous pouvez
il peut	ils peuvent

Past participle: **pu**
Passé composé: **j'ai pu**
Common noun form:
　le pouvoir *power*

VOULOIR *to want*

je veux	nous voulons
tu veux	vous voulez
il veut	ils veulent

Past participle: **voulu**
Passé composé: **j'ai voulu**

CONNAÎTRE *to know,*[17] *to be acquainted with*

je connais	nous connaissons
tu connais	vous connaissez
il connaît	ils connaissent

Past participle: **connu**[18]
Passé composé: **j'ai connu**
Common noun form:
　la connaissance *knowledge*[19]
Like **connaître:**
apparaître *to appear*
disparaître *to disappear*
paraître *to seem, to appear*
reconnaître *to recognize*

---

[14] The imperative of **dire** is: **dis, disons, dites.**

[15] There is one exception: the second person plural of **contredire, interdire,** and **prédire** becomes: **vous contredisez, vous interdisez, vous prédisez.**

[16] Unlike *can* and *may,* **pouvoir** can be conjugated in all tenses.

[17] For the difference between **connaître** and **savoir:** *to know (a fact), to know how,* see Chap. VII, note 11.

[18] **Connu:** *known* is often used as an adjective; for example: **ce fait est bien connu:** *this fact is well-known.* Cf. **inconnu:** *unknown, mysterious;* **l'inconnu:** *the unknown;* **un inconnu:** *a stranger.*

[19] Cf. **la naissance** (*birth*), **renaissance** (*rebirth*). When one gains *knowledge,* one is *born* spiritually.

⟨ CHAPTER VI ⟩

A. REFLEXIVE VERBS

PURELY REFLEXIVE VERBS

A reflexive verb has two characteristics: (1) it is accompanied by a direct object pronoun, and (2) the direct object pronoun and the subject of the verb represent the same person or thing. For instance, in **l'enfant se lave:** *the child washes* (*himself*), the pronoun **se** (*himself*) and **l'enfant** stand for the same person. (Obviously the same verbs can be used either reflexively or nonreflexively [cf. **il lave l'auto:** *he washes the car*].)

§6.2   REFLEXIVE PRONOUNS

Reflexive pronouns should be studied within a simple example:

je	me	lave *I wash* (*myself*)
tu	te	laves *etc.*
il	se	lave
elle	se	lave
nous	nous	lavons
vous	vous	lavez
ils	se	lavent

NOTE

1. Reflexive pronouns precede the verb (except in the affirmative imperative). When the verb begins with a vowel sound, **me, te, se** become **m', t', s'.**

2. When the verb is in the affirmative imperative, the reflexive pronoun follows. **Me** and **te** become **moi** and **toi** (cf. §5.5).

Couche-toi. *Lie down.*   **Levez-vous.** *Get up.*

§6.3   MEANING AND TRANSLATION

Every time the subject performs an action upon himself, French uses a reflexive pronoun. Usually this pronoun should not be translated.

Je me couche à dix heures.	*I go to bed at ten o'clock.*
Paul s'habille.	*Paul is getting dressed.*
Nous nous reposons le dimanche.[1]	*We rest on Sundays.*

A reflexive verb can also be followed by a direct object.

Elle se lave les mains.	*She washes her hands.*[2]
Il se construit une maison.	*He is building a house for himself.*

The reflexive pronoun is not emphatic. When the identity of the object must be stressed, an emphatic reflexive pronoun is added after the verb.

je me lave	moi-même[3]	*I wash myself, by myself*
tu te laves	toi-même	*you wash yourself*
il se lave	lui-même	*he washes himself*
elle se lave	elle-même	*she washes herself*
on se lave	soi-même[4]	*people wash themselves*
nous nous lavons	nous-mêmes	*we wash ourselves*
vous vous lavez	vous-même(s)	*you wash yourself, yourselves*
ils se lavent	eux-mêmes	*they wash themselves*
elles se lavent	elles-mêmes	*they wash themselves*

§6.4   RECIPROCAL VERBS

A reciprocal verb has the same characteristics as a reflexive verb, but it expresses an action done by two or more agents, one upon the other. It can be constructed with a plural subject or with **on.**

---

[1] When the names of the days of the week are preceded by an article, they indicate a regular repetition. Cf. **il a téléphoné lundi:** *he called on Monday;* **il téléphone le lundi:** *he calls on Mondays.*

[2] In this case, the subject acts upon the object (**les mains**) and the action (**laver**) is reflected back upon the subject (by means of the **se**).

[3] Depending on its position, the word **même** can have several meanings: *self, same, even, very* (i.e., *selfsame*). (See §14.8.)

[4] **Soi:** *oneself* is found in impersonal sentences; for example: **chacun pour soi:** *each one for himself.*

Les deux hommes se regardent.	*The two men look at each other.*
Mon frère et moi, nous[5] nous comprenons bien.	*My brother and I understand each other well.*
Dans ma famille, on se voit souvent.	*In my family, we see each other often.*

The context normally indicates whether the action is reflexive or reciprocal.

Les étudiants se rencontrent souvent au cinéma.	*Students often meet at the movies.* (reciprocal)
Les hommes se rasent le matin.	*Men shave in the morning.* (reflexive)

When emphasis is desired, the reciprocal pronoun can be reinforced by: **l'un l'autre:** *each other;* **les uns les autres:** *one another;* **mutuellement:** *mutually,* etc.

Les habitants de ce village s'aident les uns les autres.	*The inhabitants of this village help one another.*

§6.5   PRONOMINAL VERBS

Many French verbs are constructed with a reflexive pronoun, and yet it is often impossible to detect a reflexive meaning. In this case the verb is called pronominal; it forms, with the reflexive pronoun, an idiomatic expression. The meaning of pronominal verbs should be checked carefully, because often it is quite different from the basic meaning of the verb. The most important are:

aller *to go*	**s'en aller** *to leave, to go away*[6]
apercevoir *to perceive*	**s'apercevoir** *to become aware*
appeler *to call*	**s'appeler** *to be called, to be named*[7]
attaquer *to attack*	**s'attaquer à** *to tackle (a problem)*
attendre *to wait*	**s'attendre à** *to expect, to anticipate*[8]
demander *to ask*	**se demander** *to wonder*
douter *to doubt*	**se douter** *to suspect*
effrayer *to scare*	**s'effrayer** *to be frightened*
ennuyer *to annoy*	**s'ennuyer** *to be bored*
entendre *to hear;* (seldom) *to understand*	**s'entendre** *to agree*
étonner *to surprise*	**s'étonner** *to be surprised*
lever *to raise*	**se lever** *to rise, to get up*

[5] See §5.17. French usually repeats the two subjects by means of a plural subject pronoun.
[6] **S'en aller** and **partir** both mean *to leave, to go away.*
[7] For example: **Je m'appelle Pierre:** *My name is Peter* (lit., *I call myself Peter*).
[8] For example: **Il s'attend à une catastrophe:** *He anticipates a catastrophe.*

mettre *to put, to place*	**se mettre à** *to begin, to start*
passer *to pass*	**se passer** *to happen;* **se passer de** *to do without*[9]
plaindre *to pity*	**se plaindre** *to complain*
promener *to take for a walk*	**se promener** *to take a walk*
rappeler *to call back*	**se rappeler** *to remember, to recall*
rendre *to return, to render*	**se rendre à** *to go to*[10]
résoudre *to solve*	**se résoudre à** *to make up one's mind*
servir *to serve*	**se servir de** *to use*
tenir *to hold, to keep*	**se tenir** *to remain, to stand*
tromper *to mislead, to trick*	**se tromper** *to make a mistake*
trouver *to find*	**se trouver** *to be located, to be, to stand*

A few verbs are always accompanied by a reflexive pronoun. The most important are:

s'abstenir *to abstain, to refrain*	**se méfier de** *to distrust*
s'efforcer de *to try*	**se moquer de** *to mock*
s'emparer de *to lay hold of, to take*	**se rebeller** *to rebel*
s'enfuir *to escape*	**se repentir** *to repent*
s'envoler *to fly away*	**se soucier de** *to care for*
s'évanouir *to faint*	**se souvenir de** *to remember*
se fier à *to trust*	**se suicider** *to commit suicide*
se lamenter *to lament*	**se taire** *to keep silent*

§6.6   Verbs with a Passive Meaning

In many cases a verb constructed with the reflexive pronoun is neither reflexive nor reciprocal and yet is not pronominal.

Le Mont Blanc se voit de Chamonix.	*Mont Blanc is seen (can be seen) from Chamonix.*
Les roses se vendent deux francs la douzaine.	*Roses sell (are sold) for two francs a dozen.*
Ces moteurs se fabriquent à Toulouse.	*These motors are manufactured in Toulouse.*

It is obvious that Mont Blanc does not see, roses do not sell, and motors do not manufacture. In these sentences the verb should normally be translated by the passive in English. This construction is very common in French. It indicates that the action is done (or can be done) by

---

[9] For example: **Qu'est-ce qui se passe?** *What is going on?* **On ne peut pas se passer d'eau:** *You can't do without water.*

[10] For example: **Chaque jour il se rend à la gare:** *Every day he goes to the station.* This expression should not be confused with **se rendre compte:** *to realize* (lit., *to render to oneself an account*). For example: **Je me rends compte que la situation est grave:** *I realize that the situation is serious.* N.B.: **réaliser** means *to achieve, to accomplish.* It comes from the adjective **réel:** *real.*

unspecified agents. For instance, anyone in Chamonix can see Mont Blanc. A similar idea can be expressed with the subject pronoun **on**.

Les livres se vendent à la librairie.
On vend les livres à la librairie. } *Books are sold at the bookstore.*

B. ORTHOGRAPHICAL CHANGES
OF CERTAIN VERBS

The verbs we are going to consider here are regular verbs of the first group. However, their stems must undergo certain orthographical changes so that the spelling will correspond to the pronunciation.

1. *Verbs ending in the infinitive in* **-cer.** The c changes to ç when the ending of the verb begins with *a, o,* or *u* (see Introduction). For example: **commencer:** *to begin.*

je commence	nous commençons
tu commences	vous commencez
il commence	ils commencent

2. *Verbs ending in the infinitive in* **-ger.** An *e* is added after the *g* when the ending of the verb begins with *a, o,* or *u* (see Introduction). For example: **manger:** *to eat.*

je mange	nous mangeons
tu manges	vous mangez
il mange	ils mangent

3. *Verbs ending in the infinitive in* **-eter** *and* **-eler.** In most cases, the *t* or the *l* is doubled when the ending of the verb begins with a mute *e*. For example: **appeler:** *to call.*

j'appelle	nous appelons
tu appelles	vous appelez
il appelle	ils appellent

Exception: **Acheter:** *to buy* and **geler:** *to freeze* change the *e* of the stem to *è* when the ending of the verb begins with a mute *e:*

j'achète	nous achetons
tu achètes	vous achetez
il achète	ils achètent

4. Verbs with an *e* in the last syllable of the stem change this *e* to *è* when the ending begins with a mute *e*. For example: **mener:** *to lead.*

je mène	nous menons
tu mènes	vous menez
il mène	ils mènent

5. Verbs with an *é* in the last syllable of the stem change this *é* to *è* when the ending begins with a mute *e*. For example: **espérer:** *to hope*.

j'espère	nous espérons
tu espères	vous espérez
il espère	ils espèrent

IRREGULAR PRESENTS
AND PAST PARTICIPLES

APERCEVOIR *to perceive*

j'aperçois[11]	nous apercevons
tu aperçois	vous apercevez
il aperçoit	ils aperçoivent

Past participle: **aperçu**
Passé composé: **j'ai aperçu**
Verbs conjugated like **apercevoir:**
concevoir *to conceive*
décevoir *to disappoint*
recevoir *to receive*

CRAINDRE *to fear*

je crains	nous craignons
tu crains	vous craignez
il craint	ils craignent

Past participle: **craint**
Passé composé: **j'ai craint**
Common noun form:
   la crainte *fear*
Like **craindre:** all verbs in **-indre**
   The most common are:
atteindre *to reach, to attain*
éteindre *to put out, to extinguish*
joindre *to join*
peindre *to paint*
plaindre *to pity*
rejoindre *to rejoin, to overtake*

---

[11] Note the *ç*. Cf. §6.7.

⊫ CHAPTER VII ⊐

A. NEGATIVE SENTENCES

BASIC FORM

In a negative sentence the verb is preceded by **ne** and generally followed by **pas**.[1]

Il parle.	*He speaks*
Il ne parle pas.	*He does not speak.*

NOTE

1. **Ne** becomes **n'** when the following word begins with a vowel sound.

Il n'étudie pas.	*He does not study.*

2. **Ne** is common to all negations. **Pas,** however, can be replaced by other negative particles (see §7.2).

3. In French, no auxiliary (such as *do*) is ever used to form a negation.

§7.2 OTHER FORMS

Ne . . . point[2] (*not*)

Il ne voit point.	*He doesn't see.*

---

[1] Originally the negation was formed with the single word: **ne**. Then, with verbs of motion, such as **aller:** *to go,* people began to add the word **un pas:** *a step:* **je ne vais (un) pas:** *I don't go (a) step.* The basic meaning of **pas** in this construction was soon forgotten and gradually the negation **ne . . . pas** was used with all verbs.

[2] Literally, **un point:** *a stitch.* Originally this negation was used with verbs such as **coudre:** *to sew.*

Ne . . . _personne_ (nobody)

Il ne voit personne.   *He doesn't see anyone.*

Ne . . . _rien_ (nothing)

Il ne voit rien.   *He doesn't see anything (he sees nothing).*

Ne . . . _plus_ (no longer, no more)

Il ne lit plus.   *He is no longer reading. He doesn't read any more.*

Ne . . . _jamais_ (never)

Il ne lit jamais.   *He never reads.*

Ne . . . _guère_ (hardly, scarcely)

Il ne mange guère.   *He hardly eats.*

Ne . . . _aucun(e)_ + _noun_ (no)

Il ne voit aucun danger.   *He doesn't see any danger (he sees no danger).*

Ne . . . _nul(le)_ + _noun_ (no)

Il n'a nulle autorité.   *He has no authority.*

Ne . . . _ni_ . . . _ni_ (neither . . . nor)

Il n'a ni frère ni sœur.   *He has neither (a) brother nor (a) sister.*

Ne . . . _que_ (only, nothing but)

Il n'a que dix francs.   *He has only ten francs.*

§7.3 **NOTE**

1. **Ne . . . pas** and **ne . . . point** have the same meaning. **Ne . . . point** is more literary and somewhat archaic.

2. The negation **ne . . . personne** must not be confused with the noun **la personne**: *person.* To avoid confusion, remember that a negation is always accompanied by **ne**.

Je vois une personne.   *I see a (one) person.*
Je ne vois personne.   *I don't see anyone.*

3. The negation **ne . . . plus** indicates that an action has been sus-

pended. It must not be confused with **plus:** *more* or **le plus:** *the most* (see §§2.18, 2.21).

J'ai plus de travail que Paul.	*I have more work than Paul.*
Je n'ai plus de travail.	*I don't have any more work (I have no more work).*

4. **Ne . . . guère** indicates a small number or amount.

Il n'a guère d'argent.	*He has hardly any money.*

5. Of the negative forms, only **aucun** and **nul** are adjectives and agree with the following noun.

Il n'a aucune ambition.	*He has no ambition.*

6. **Ne . . . que** is *not* a negation; it indicates a limit or restriction and is translated with *only, nothing but, nothing except* and a verb in the affirmative.

Il n'a qu'un frère.	*He has only one brother.*
Nous n'avons qu'une heure.	*We have only an (one) hour.*

§7.4 POSITION OF NEGATIVE PARTICLES

1. When the verb is in a compound tense, the negative particles frame the auxiliary.

Je n'ai pas fini.	*I haven't finished.*
Il n'a jamais voyagé.	*He has never travelled.*

2. When the verb is accompanied by one or two object pronouns, **ne** precedes the object pronouns.

Il ne la voit jamais.	*He never sees her (it).*
Je ne le lui ai pas donné.	*I didn't give it to him (her).*

3. When the verb is in the imperative, the two negative particles are placed in their usual position.

Ne venez pas.	*Don't come.*
Ne lui parlez pas.	*Don't talk to him (her).*

4. When the verb is in the infinitive, the two negative particles precede.

Ne pas manger de viande est mauvais pour la santé.	*Not to eat (any) meat is bad for the health.*

5. Certain negations can be subjects. In this case, the negative particle, which normally follows the verb, stands at the beginning of the clause.

Personne ne vient.	*No one is coming.*
Rien ne bouge.	*Nothing is moving.*
Aucun homme ne peut tout savoir.	*No man can know everything.*
Nul homme n'est infaillible.	*No man is infallible.*

Ne Used Alone

In literary French, **ne** may be found without the **pas**. This construction appears mostly in clauses beginning with **si**: *if* or in those containing the verbs **pouvoir**: *can, to be able,* **savoir**: *to know,* **cesser**: *to stop, to cease,* **oser**: *to dare.*[3]

S'il ne m'aide (pas) je suis perdu.	*If he doesn't help me I'm lost.*
Il ne sait (pas) où aller.	*He doesn't know where to go.*
Je ne peux (pas) faire cela.	*I can't do that.*

*Complex Negatives

A verb can be accompanied by two, or even three negatives. The same **ne** is used for all of them. Since double negatives are not possible in English, the translation of these sentences is difficult. Each element of the French sentence must be carefully analyzed before attempting a translation. Here are the possible complex negations:

ne . . . pas que

Il ne parle pas que le français; il parle aussi l'espagnol.	*He not only speaks French; he also speaks Spanish.*

ne . . . guère que

Dans ce désert, je ne vois guère que des cactus.	*In this desert, I see almost nothing but cactuses.*

ne . . . rien que

Le lion ne mange rien que de la viande.	*The lion doesn't eat anything but meat.*

---

[3] Negative sentences formed with **ne** alone must not be confused with other literary sentences that contain a superfluous **ne**. This particular use of **ne** is limited to a few specific cases (see §14.6).

* The complex constructions in §7.6 are not so very common that a beginner needs to study them in depth. However, when you start reading, beware of them because, when they do occur, they change the meaning of a sentence.

ne . . . plus personne

Le soir, il n'y a plus personne ici.

In the evening, there is no longer anyone here.

ne . . . plus rien

Quand je suis fatigué, je ne fais plus rien.

When I am tired, I don't do anything more.

ne . . . plus que

Il a beaucoup dépensé; il n'a plus que dix francs.

He has spent a great deal; he has only ten francs left.

ne . . . plus aucun

N'ayez pas peur; il n'y a plus aucun danger.

Don't be afraid; there's no more danger.

ne . . . plus guère

Il n'y a plus guère de clients.

There are almost no (hardly any) customers left.

ne . . . jamais plus

Caruso est mort; il ne chantera jamais plus.

Caruso is dead; he will never sing again (anymore).

ne . . . jamais personne

Il ne voit jamais personne.

He never sees anyone.

ne . . . jamais rien

Il ne donne jamais rien.

He never gives anything.

ne . . . jamais que

Dans ce restaurant je ne vois jamais que quelques clients.

In this restaurant, I never see more than a few customers.

ne . . . jamais aucun

Il ne fait jamais aucune faute.

He never makes a single mistake.

ne . . . jamais guère

Il n'a jamais guère d'appétit.

He hardly ever has any appetite.

ne . . . jamais plus personne

Il ne voit jamais plus personne. *He never sees anyone anymore.*

ne . . . jamais plus rien

Il ne dit jamais plus rien. *He never says anything anymore.*

ne . . . jamais plus que

Ce musicien ne joue jamais plus que de la musique classique. *This musician never plays anything anymore except classical music.*

B. RELATIVE PRONOUNS

§7.7

A relative pronoun links two clauses. For example: **Je vois le livre** + **le livre est sur la table** → **Je vois le livre qui est sur la table:** *I see the book (which is) on the table.*

In this sentence, the relative pronoun **qui** replaces the noun, **le livre,** which is called the antecedent. Usually the antecedent precedes the relative pronoun.

§7.8

SUBJECT PRONOUN QUI

The relative pronoun **qui** stands for either persons or things.[4] Since it is a subject, it is generally followed directly by the verb. Normally **qui** should be translated by *who* or *which*. Sometimes no relative pronoun is necessary in the English sentence; in French it cannot be omitted.

Je vois l'homme qui parle. *I see the man who is speaking.*
Les papiers qui sont sur mon bureau sont importants. *The papers (that are) on my desk are important.*

---

[4] Be careful not to confuse relative pronouns with interrogative pronouns. When **qui** is an interrogative pronoun, it refers only to persons. Cf. Tables 4.2 and 7.1.

The relative pronoun **que** stands for either persons or things.[5] Since it is a direct object, it is generally followed by the subject of the verb. **Que** should usually be translated by: *whom, which,* or *that.* Sometimes no relative pronoun is necessary in the English sentence; in French, once again, it cannot be omitted.

L'étudiant que vous avez vu étudie l'histoire.	*The student whom you have seen studies history.*
Voici un livre que je veux acheter.	*Here is a book (that) I want to buy.*

NOTE

The subject pronoun **qui** and the object pronoun **que** should not be confused. Let us compare:

Je vois le livre qui est sur le bureau.	*I see the book (that is) on the desk.*
Je vois le livre que Paul lit.	*I see the book that Paul is reading.*

OBJECTS OF PREPOSITIONS

§7.10   1. *Preposition + qui (for persons only).* Any preposition (except **de**) can be followed by **qui;**[6] the usual translation is: preposition + *whom.*

L'ami à qui j'écris habite à Paris.	*The friend to whom I am writing lives in Paris.*
Je connais le monsieur avec qui elle parle.	*I know the gentleman with whom she is talking.*

§7.11   2. *Preposition + lequel (generally for things).* Any preposition can be followed by **lequel;**[7] the usual translation is: preposition + *which.* **Lequel** is the only relative pronoun that agrees with the noun which it represents.

	SINGULAR	PLURAL
M.	lequel	lesquels
F.	laquelle	lesquelles

When **lequel** is preceded by the preposition **à,** the two words contract in

---

[5] Again, do not confuse it with the interrogative pronoun **que.**

[6] Note that in *interrogative* sentences, **de qui** is used (see §4.12).

[7] The relative pronouns **duquel, de laquelle, desquels, desquelles** are seldom used except in legal matters.

the masculine singular and in the plural: **auquel, à laquelle, auxquels, auxquelles** (cf. §4.2).

Voici la machine avec laquelle nous travaillons.	*Here is the machine with which we work.*
La compagnie pour laquelle il travaille est en déficit.	*The company for which he works is losing money.*
Le tableau auquel vous pensez[8] est au Louvre.	*The painting (that) you are thinking about is in the Louvre.*

§7.12   3. ***Dont*** (*for persons or things*). **Dont** is never preceded by a preposition because it stands for two words: preposition **de** + relative pronoun. The translation of **dont** is thus linked to the various meanings of **de** (see §§4.4-4.7); usually it can be rendered by: *from which, from whom, of which, whose, about which, about whom.*

Il a publié les résultats dont il est certain.	*He has published the results of which he is certain.*
Il achète les livres dont il a besoin.[9]	*He buys the books that he needs (lit., of which he has need).*
Je n'ai pas vu le film dont vous parlez.	*I haven't seen the movie (that) you are talking about (lit., about which you are talking).*
Debussy est un compositeur dont je reconnais immédiatement le style.	*Debussy is a composer whose style I recognize immediately.[10]*

§7.13   4. ***Où*** (*for things only*). **Où** is used to refer to a location or a specific moment. Its usual translation is *where* or *when*.

Le village où il habite est pittoresque.	*The village where he lives is picturesque.*
J'ai vu Pierre juste au moment où il a ouvert la porte.	*I saw Peter just when he opened the door.[11]*

D'où refers to the origin or cause. Its usual translations are *from which* or *hence*.

Il est fatigué, d'où son mauvais travail.	*He is tired, hence his bad work.*

§7.14   For a convenient table of the relative pronouns, see Table 7.1.

---

[8] **Penser à:** *to think of, to think about;* **penser de:** *to think of, to have an opinion about.*

[9] See §7.17.

[10] When the object comes after **dont,** the French sentence follows the usual order: subject + verb + object. In the equivalent English sentence, after *whose* the word order becomes: object + subject + verb.

[11] When **où** is used to mean *when,* it is always preceded by a noun of time (**l'heure:** *hour;* **le jour:** *day,* etc.). Otherwise the conjunction **quand:** *when* is used. Cf. **J'ai vu Pierre quand il a ouvert la porte:** *I saw Peter when he opened the door.*

TABLE 7.1

RELATIVE PRONOUNS

	PERSONS	THINGS
SUBJECT	qui *who* L'homme qui est ici. *The man who is here.*	qui *which, that* Le livre qui est ici. *The book that is here.*
DIRECT OBJECT	que *whom, that* L'homme que je vois. *The man whom I see.*	que *which, that* Le livre que je lis. *The book that I read.*
INDIRECT OBJECT (*object of a preposition*)	I prep. + qui *whom* L'homme avec qui il parle. *The man with whom he is speaking.*	I prep. + lequel *which* Le crayon avec lequel il écrit. *The pencil with which he is writing.*
	II dont *of whom, about whom* L'homme dont il parle. *The man about whom he is talking.*	II dont *of which, about which* Le livre dont il parle. *The book about which he is talking.*
		III où *where, when* La ville où il habite. *The town where he lives.* Le jour où je le vois. *The day when I see him.*

C. POSSESSIVE PRONOUNS

§7.15   Like the possessive adjectives (see §§2.14-2.16), the possessive pronouns agree with the thing possessed. The possessive pronouns replace a noun; they are always preceded by an article.

The translation of the possessive pronouns presents no difficulties except in the case of the third person singular. In French, these pronouns agree in gender and in number with the thing possessed.

Il a son livre mais elle n'a pas le sien.	*He has his book, but she does not have hers.*
Paul a sa montre mais Pierre a oublié la sienne.	*Paul has his watch, but Peter has forgotten his.*

§7.16   For a convenient listing of the possessive pronouns, see Table 7.2.

TABLE 7.2

POSSESSIVE PRONOUNS

GENDER AND NUMBER OF THINGS POSSESSED

	MASCULINE SINGULAR	FEMININE SINGULAR	MASCULINE PLURAL	FEMININE PLURAL	ENGLISH TRANSLATION
1 P. SG.	le mien	la mienne	les miens	les miennes	*mine*
2 P. SG.	le tien	la tienne	les tiens	les tiennes	*yours*
3 P. SG. M.	le sien	la sienne	les siens	les siennes	*his/hers/its*
——— F.	le sien	la sienne	les siens	les siennes	*his/hers/its*
1 P. PL.	le nôtre	la nôtre	les nôtres	les nôtres	*ours*
2 P. PL.	le vôtre	la vôtre	les vôtres	les vôtres	*yours*
3 P. PL. (M&F)	le leur	la leur	les leurs	les leurs	*theirs*

§7.17   **IDIOMATIC EXPRESSIONS FORMED WITH AVOIR**

Several idiomatic expressions are formed with **avoir** + noun. Most of them should be translated in English with *to be* + adjective.

NOUN	IDIOMATIC EXPRESSION	TRANSLATION
la faim *hunger*	**avoir faim**	*to be hungry*
la soif *thirst*	**avoir soif**	*to be thirsty*
le chaud *heat*	**avoir chaud**	*to be hot*

	IDIOMATIC	
NOUN	EXPRESSION	TRANSLATION
le froid *cold*	avoir froid	*to be cold*
l'envie *desire*	avoir envie de	*to desire, to wish*
la peur *fear*	avoir peur de	*to be afraid of*
le besoin *need*	avoir besoin de	*to need*
le lieu *place*	avoir lieu	*to take place*
la honte *shame*	avoir honte de	*to be ashamed of*

§7.18

IRREGULAR PRESENTS AND PAST PARTICIPLES

DEVOIR *must, to have to, to owe*[12]

je dois	nous devons
tu dois	vous devez
il doit	ils doivent

Past participle: **dû**
Passé composé: **j'ai dû**
Common noun form:
 le devoir *duty*

SAVOIR *to know, to know how*[13]

je sais	nous savons
tu sais	vous savez
il sait	ils savent

Past participle: **su**
Passé composé: **j'ai su**

---

[12] **Devoir** is irregular, but it can be conjugated in all tenses (see §14.7).

[13] Both **connaître** and **savoir** are usually translated by *to know* (see §5.21). Normally **savoir** is used to express the knowledge of a precise fact, while **connaître** is used to express acquaintance or general knowledge that consists of several facts. For example: **Je sais où Paul habite:** *I know where Paul lives;* **je connais cet homme:** *I know this man;* **je connais l'histoire des Etats-Unis:** *I know the history of the United States;* **Savoir** + infinitive means *to know how;* for example: **il sait lire:** *he knows how to read* (see §13.7).

⌈⊩ CHAPTER VIII ⊪⌉

A. THE IMPERFECT TENSE

§8.1   The imperfect (*l'imparfait*) is a simple tense (i.e., formed without an auxiliary). It is formed by adding to the stem the following endings:

FIRST GROUP		SECOND GROUP		THIRD GROUP	
marcher		finir		vendre	
je march	ais	je fin	issais	je vend	ais
tu march	ais	tu fin	issais	tu vend	ais
il march	ait	il fin	issait	il vend	ait
nous march	ions	nous fin	issions	nous vend	ions
vous march	iez	vous fin	issiez	vous vend	iez
ils march	aient	ils fin	issaient	ils vend	aient

NOTE

1. All imperfect endings contain either **ai** or **i**.

2. The endings of the three groups are identical, but in the second group, the particle **iss** is inserted between the stem and the ending.

§8.2   IRREGULAR IMPERFECTS

The *endings* of the imperfect are always regular; the stem of certain verbs, however, undergoes slight changes:

	INFINITIVE	IRREGULAR PART OF STEM	IMPERFECT
atteindre *to reach* plaindre *to pity*		-gn[1]	j'atteignais je plaignais
prendre *to take* apprendre *to learn* comprendre *to understand* entreprendre *to undertake* surprendre *to surprise*		-n[2]	je prenais j'apprenais je comprenais j'entreprenais je surprenais
dire *to tell* lire *to read* faire *to make* plaire *to please* conduire *to drive, to lead* construire *to build* déduire *to deduce, to deduct* détruire *to destroy* instruire *to instruct* produire *to produce*		-s	je disais je lisais je faisais je plaisais je conduisais je construisais je déduisais je détruisais j'instruisais je produisais
paraître *to seem, to appear* apparaître *to appear* naître *to be born* connaître *to know*		-ss	je paraissais j'apparaissais je naissais je connaissais
boire *to drink* écrire *to write*		-v	je buvais j'écrivais

The imperfect of **avoir** is regular: **j'avais,** etc. The imperfect of **être** is also regular, except for the accent: **j'étais, tu étais, il était,** etc.

§8.3   ### MEANINGS AND TRANSLATIONS

Like the passé composé (§3.12), the imperfect is a past tense. However, the meanings of the two tenses are radically different.

§8.4   1. *The imperfect describes past situations.* It can describe environment, background, or physical or moral characteristics. Usually it should be translated by the English past tense or by a progressive form in the past:

Ce matin le ciel était bleu.	*This morning the sky was blue.*
Mon grand-père était médecin.	*My grandfather was a doctor.*
Hier Paul était malade.	*Yesterday Paul was sick.*
Les rois de France habitaient au Louvre.	*The kings of France lived (used to live) in the Louvre.*[3]

---

[1] All verbs in **-indre** are conjugated like **atteindre** and **plaindre.** (Cf. §6.8.)
[2] Cf. §3.10.
[3] See Table 8.1.

§8.5   2. *The imperfect expresses habits or actions that have been repeated an indefinite number of times.* Usually it should be translated by the English past tense or by expressions such as *used to* or *was in the habit of.*

Churchill fumait de gros cigars.	*Churchill used to smoke big cigars.*
Quand j'étais à Paris, j'allais souvent à l'Opéra.	*When I was in Paris, I often went to the Opera.*
Pasteur vérifiait le résultat de ses expériences plusieurs fois.	*Pasteur used to check the result of his experiments several times.*

§8.6   3. *The imperfect expresses actions that were in progress at a certain moment.* It presents the actions in the course of their development, when they were still unfinished.[4] On the other hand, the passé composé presents the actions as completed, whether they lasted for a brief moment or for a long period; it states final results.

The imperfect and the passé composé are often used in contrast:

Il lisait quand elle l'a appelé.	*He was reading when she called him.*
Les alpinistes montaient vers le sommet de la montagne quand l'orage a éclaté.	*The alpinists were climbing toward the summit of the mountain when the storm broke out.[5]*

B. THE PAST DEFINITE

§8.7   The past definite (*le passé défini* or *passé simple*) is a literary tense. It is almost never used in speech but is found constantly in written French. It, too, is a simple tense, formed by adding to the stem the following endings:

FIRST GROUP		SECOND GROUP		THIRD GROUP			
marcher		finir		vendre *(used for most verbs in -re)*		mourir *(used for most verbs in -ir, -oir)*	
je march	ai	je fin	is	je vend	is	je mour	us
tu march	as	tu fin	is	tu vend	is	tu mour	us
il march	a	il fin	it	il vend	it	il mour	ut
nous march	âmes	nous fin	îmes	nous vend	îmes	nous mour	ûmes
vous march	âtes	vous fin	îtes	vous vend	îtes	vous mour	ûtes
ils march	èrent	ils fin	irent	ils vend	irent	ils mour	urent

[4] The basic meaning of **imparfait** means *unfinished, not perfected.*
[5] See Table 8.1.

Many verbs of the third group are irregular in the past definite. It is helpful to remember that all have in common at least the last part of the ending: **-s, -s, -t, ⁀mes, ⁀tes, -rent.** Students should learn to recognize the past definite of the most common irregular verbs (see §8.22 and Appendix C).

§8.9   MEANING AND TRANSLATION

The past definite and the passé composé are identical in meaning. Both present completed actions. The past definite is unusual in conversational French; however, many writers prefer it for stylistic reasons. Since it is formal and literary, the past definite is used mostly in the third person singular and plural. The normal translation of the past definite is the English past tense.

Guillaume le Conquérant battit Harold.	*William the Conqueror fought Harold.*
L'assassin tira et partit.	*The murderer shot and left.*
Montgolfier construisit les premiers ballons.	*Montgolfier built the first balloons.*

C. AUXILIARY ÊTRE AND AVOIR

§8.10   Compound tenses such as the passé composé (see §3.11) are formed with an auxiliary and the past participle of the verb. Most verbs are conjugated with the auxiliary **avoir.**

§8.11   VERBS CONJUGATED WITH AVOIR

All verbs that can have a direct object (i.e., transitive verbs) use the auxiliary **avoir.**

J'écris une lettre.	*I write a letter.*	→ **J'ai écrit.**	*I wrote.*
Je prends un livre.	*I take a book.*	→ **J'ai pris.**	*I took.*

NOTE

Certain verbs are transitive in French and intransitive in English, or vice versa. For example: **regarder:** *to look at;* **écouter:** *to listen to:*

Je regarde la maison.	*I look at the house.*
J'écoute la musique.	*I listen to the music.*

Two categories of verbs use the auxiliary **être**: (1) All reflexive and reciprocal verbs, and (2) a group of nineteen intransitive verbs.

§8.13   1. *Reflexive and reciprocal verbs.* Most French verbs can be used with a reflexive pronoun (see Chap. VI) and thus become reflexive or reciprocal, in which case they are conjugated with the auxiliary **être**.

PRESENT		PASSÉ COMPOSÉ	
Je lave l'enfant.	*I wash the child.*	**J'ai lavé l'enfant.**	*I washed the child.*
Je me lave.	*I wash (myself).*	**Je me suis lavé.**	*I washed (myself).*
Je vois mon ami.	*I see my friend.*	**J'ai vu mon ami.**	*I saw my friend.*
Ils se voient.	*They see each other.*	**Ils se sont vus.**	*They saw each other.*

NOTE

Reflexive verbs must not be confused with the passive voice (see §13.14) or with adjectives used predicatively. A reflexive verb is *always* accompanied by a reflexive pronoun. A verb in the passive or an adjective is never accompanied by a reflexive pronoun. For instance:

Il s'est assis.	*He sat down.*	**Il est assis.**	*He is sitting.*
Il s'est reposé.	*He rested.*	**Il est reposé.**	*He is rested.*
Il s'est couché.	*He went to bed.*	**Il est couché.**	*He is lying down.*

§8.14   2. *Certain intransitive verbs.* Nineteen intransitive verbs (i.e., that cannot have a direct object) are always conjugated with the auxiliary **être**.

(*a*) **aller:** *to go*

Je suis allé à la gare.	*I went to the station.*
Il est allé à Paris en avion.[6]	*He flew to Paris.*

(*b*) **venir:** *to come*

Il est venu au bureau.	*He came to the office.*

Several verbs formed with **venir** also use the auxiliary **être**: **revenir:** *to come back;* **devenir:** *to become;* **survenir:** *to happen, to occur;* **parvenir:** *to reach, to succeed.*

Il est revenu rapidement.	*He came back quickly.*
Il est devenu architecte.[7]	*He became an architect.*

---

[6] Note that **aller** is always used with a preposition except when immediately followed by the infinitive. (See §§3.9 and 10.1.)

[7] In this case, the noun **architecte** is not the object of the verb; it plays the part of an adjective. Cf. **il est devenu célèbre:** *he became famous.*

L'accident est survenu hier.	*The accident happened yesterday.*
Il est parvenu au sommet.	*He reached the summit.*

(*c*) **arriver:** *to arrive; to happen*

Il est arrivé à huit heures.	*He arrived at eight o'clock.*
L'accident est arrivé hier.	*The accident happened yesterday.*
Qu'est-ce qui est arrivé?	*What (has) happened?*

(*d*) **partir:** *to leave, to start off* [8]

Le train est parti.	*The train (has) left.*
Je suis parti à midi.	*I left at noon.*

(*e*) **rester:** *to stay, to remain* [9]

Hier je suis resté à la maison.	*Yesterday I stayed home.*

(*f*) **retourner:** *to go back*

Il est retourné à l'hôpital.	*He went back to the hospital.*

(*g*) **tomber:** *to fall*

Il est tombé sur les marches.	*He fell on the steps.*
Gauguin est tombé dans la misère.	*Gauguin fell into misery.*

(*h*) **naître:** *to be born*

Paul est né à Paris.	*Paul was born in Paris.*
Il est né dans la misère.	*He was born in poverty.*

(*i*) **mourir:** *to die*

Churchill est mort[10] à Londres.	*Churchill died in London.*

(*j*) **passer:** *to go by, to pass* [11]

L'auto est passée devant la maison.	*The car passed in front of the house.*

(*k*) **monter:** *to go up, to climb;* **descendre:** *to descend, to go down;* **sortir:** *to exit, to go out;* **entrer:** *to enter, to go in;* **rentrer:** *to enter, to come in; to come back, to return.*

These five verbs can be transitive or intransitive, depending on their

[8] **Partir** must not be confused with **laisser:** *to leave behind.* The latter is transitive and is therefore conjugated with **avoir.** For example: **J'ai laissé mon chien à la maison:** *I left my dog at home.*

[9] **Rester** must not be confused with **se reposer:** *to rest.* Cf. **il reste là:** *he is staying there;* **il se repose là:** *he is resting there.*

[10] The words **né** and **mort** can be either adjectives or past participles. Thus, **il est mort** can be translated by either *he is dead* or *he died.* The context normally indicates the meaning. For example: **Maintenant il est mort:** *now he is dead;* **il est mort en 1950:** *he died in 1950;* **le bébé est né:** *the baby is born;* **il est né à Paris:** *he was born in Paris.* Note too, that **la mort** means *death;* **le mort, la morte:** *dead person.*

[11] **Passer** is conjugated with **avoir** when it means *to hand over.* For example: **Il a passé le journal à la dame:** *he handed the newspaper to the lady.*

meaning. When they are transitive they are conjugated with **avoir** and have the following meaning: **monter:** *to take up, to carry up;* **descendre:** *to take down, to carry down;* **sortir:** *to carry out, to take outside;* **entrer:** *to bring in;* **rentrer:** *to bring back.*

Il a monté la valise.	*He took the suitcase upstairs.*
Il a sorti le chien.	*He took the dog out.*

When these verbs are intransitive, they have no direct object and are conjugated with **être:**

Il est monté jusqu'au sommet.	*He climbed to the top.*
Il est descendu à la cave.	*He went down to the cellar.*
Paul est sorti avec Marie.	*Paul went out with Mary.*
Ils sont rentrés à midi.	*They came back at noon.*

§8.15   For a graphic depiction of those verbs that take **être** as their auxiliary, see Fig. 8.1.

D. AGREEMENT OF PAST PARTICIPLES

§8.16   1. *Past participles of intransitive verbs conjugated with **être.*** These past participles always agree in gender and number with the subject of the verb.

Elle est venue.	*She came.*
Ils sont sortis.	*They went out.*
Elles sont arrivées.	*They arrived.*

§8.17   2. *Past participles of transitive verbs.* All transitive verbs are conjugated with the auxiliary **avoir** (see §8.13); their past participles agree in gender and number with the direct object, *if the direct object precedes* the verb. Cf.:

J'ai lu ces livres.	*I read these books.*
Les livres que j'ai lus sont intéressants.	*The books that I read are interesting.*
Avez-vous lu ces livres? Oui je les ai lus.	*Have you read these books? Yes, I've read them.*

In the first instance, **lu** precedes the direct object, **livres,** and therefore does not agree. In the second instance, the direct object precedes the verb; therefore **lus** agrees with **livres.**

§8.18   3. *Past participles of reflexive verbs.* The past participles of reflexive or reciprocal verbs agree with the reflexive pronoun:

Elle s'est levée.	*She got up.*
Les deux sœurs se sont vues.	*The two sisters saw each other.*

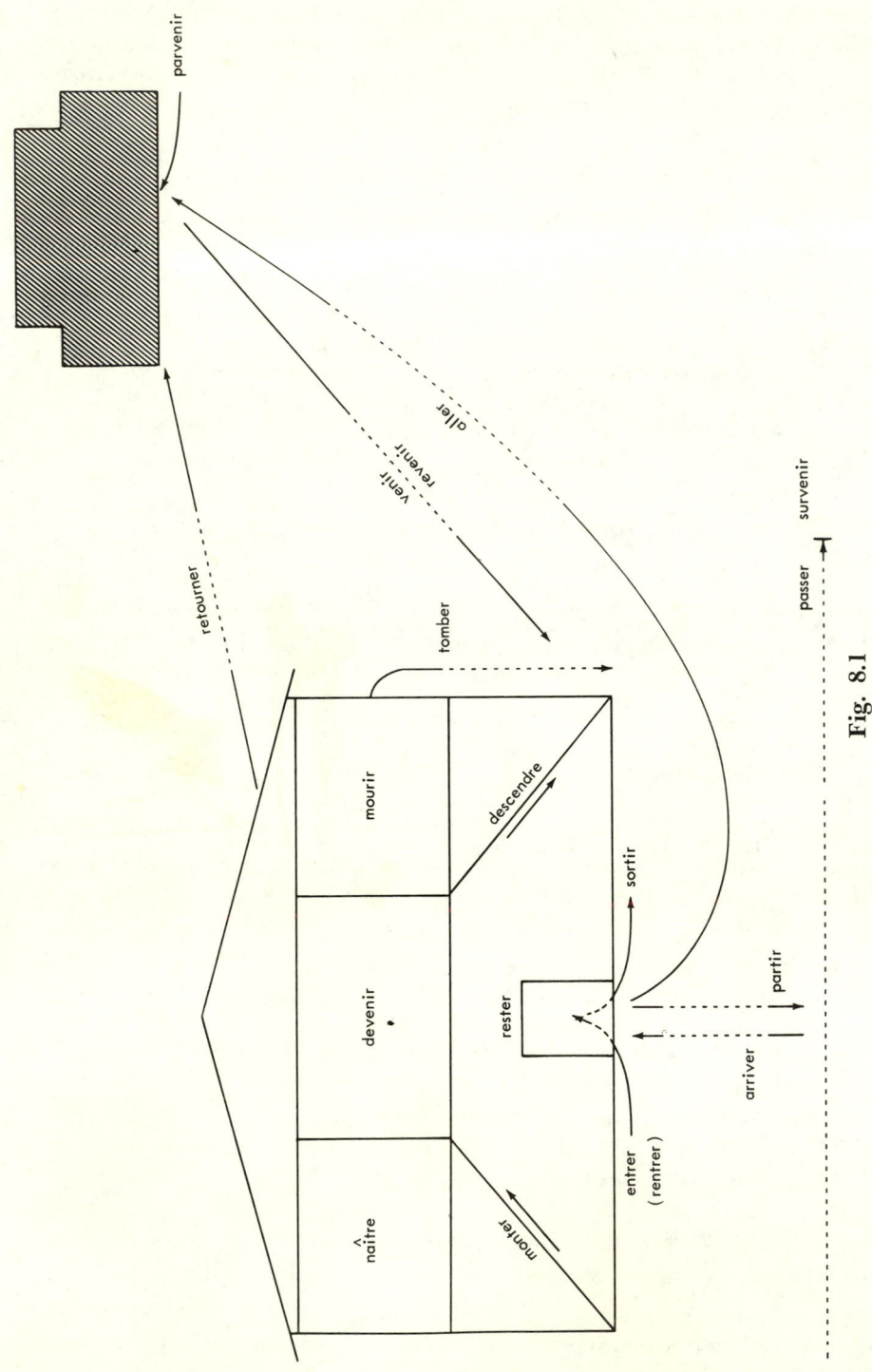

Fig. 8.1

However, when a reflexive verb is followed by a direct object, the past participle never agrees:

Elle s'est lavée.	*She washed.*
Elle s'est lavé les mains.	*She washed her hands.*[12]

§8.19

IRREGULAR PRESENTS
AND PAST PARTICIPLES

NAÎTRE *to be born*

je nais	nous naissons
tu nais	vous naissez
il naît	ils naissent

Past participle: **né**
Passé composé: **il est né**
Common noun form:
  la naissance *birth*
Like **naître:**
renaître *to revive, to be reborn*

MOURIR *to die*

je meurs	nous mourons
tu meurs	vous mourez
il meurt	ils meurent

Past participle: **mort**
Passé composé: **il est mort**
Common noun forms:
  la mort *death*
  le mort, la morte *dead person*

VENIR *to come*

je viens	nous venons
tu viens	vous venez
il vient	ils viennent

Past participle: **venu**
Passé composé: **il est venu**
Like **venir:**[13]
devenir *to become*
parvenir *to succeed*
revenir *to come back*
se souvenir *to remember*
survenir *to happen*

PARTIR *to leave, to depart*

je pars	nous partons
tu pars	vous partez
il part	ils partent

Past participle: **parti**
Passé composé: **il est parti**
Common noun form:
  le départ *departure, leaving*

VAINCRE *to conquer, to vanquish*

je vaincs	nous vainquons
tu vaincs	vous vainquez
il vainc	ils vainquent

Past participle: **vaincu**
Passé composé: **il a vaincu**
Like **vaincre:**
convaincre *to convince*

---

[12] The agreement of past participles used with reflexive verbs is one of the fine points of French grammar. The preceding information is sufficient for students seeking a reading knowledge of French.

[13] The following verbs are also conjugated like **venir,** but they use the auxiliary **avoir: tenir:** *to hold;* **appartenir:** *to belong, to pertain;* **contenir:** *to contain;* **détenir:** *to detain;* **maintenir:** *to maintain;* **retenir:** *to hold back, to retain;* **soutenir:** *to sustain.*

INFINITIVE	3 P. SG.	3 P. PL.
avoir *to have*	il eut	ils eurent
être *to be*	il fut	ils furent
dire *to say*	il dit	ils dirent
faire *to make*	il fit	ils firent
mettre *to put*[14]	il mit	ils mirent
prendre *to take*[15]	il prit	ils prirent
voir *to see*	il vit	ils virent
écrire *to write*	il écrivit	ils écrivirent
naître *to be born*	il naquit	ils naquirent
vaincre *to conquer, to vanquish*[16]	il vainquit	ils vainquirent
craindre *to fear*	il craignit	ils craignirent
plaindre *to pity*	il plaignit	ils plaignirent
atteindre *to reach*	il atteignit	ils atteignirent
construire *to build*	il construisit	ils construisirent
produire *to produce*[17]	il produisit	ils produisirent
tenir *to hold* [18]	il tint	ils tinrent
venir *to come*[19]	il vint	ils vinrent
accroître *to increase*	il accrut	ils accrurent
apercevoir *to perceive*[20]	il aperçut	ils aperçurent
boire *to drink*	il but	ils burent
connaître *to know*	il connut	ils connurent
devoir *to have to, to owe*	il dut	ils durent
lire *to read*	il lut	ils lurent
mourir *to die*	il mourut	ils moururent
plaire *to please*	il plut	ils plurent
pouvoir *to be able*	il put	ils purent
savoir *to know*	il sut	ils surent
vivre *to live*	il vécut	ils vécurent
vouloir *to want*	il voulut	ils voulurent

---

[14] Verbs conjugated like **mettre** are: **admettre, commettre, omettre, permettre, remettre, soumettre** (see §3.17).

[15] Like **prendre**: **apprendre, comprendre, entreprendre, reprendre, surprendre** (see §2.24).

[16] Like **craindre, plaindre,** and **vaincre**: all the verbs in **-indre** (see §6.8).

[17] Like **construire** and **produire**: **déduire, détruire, instruire** (see §4.16).

[18] Like **tenir**: **appartenir, contenir, détenir, maintenir, retenir, soutenir** (see §3.16).

[19] Like **venir**: **devinir, parvenir, revenir, se souvenir,** and **souvenir**.

[20] Like **apercevoir**: **concevoir, décevoir,** and **recevoir** (see §6.8).

TABLE 8.1a

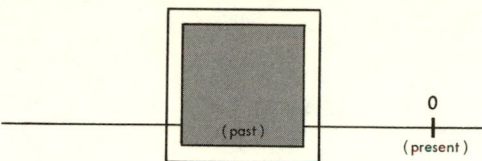

Paul était grand. *Paul was tall.*
" " **intelligent.** *Paul was intelligent.*
" " **ingénieur.** *Paul was an engineer.*
Paul habitait à Paris. *Paul lived in Paris.*
Il pleuvait. *It was raining.*
Les Romains aimaient la guerre. *The Romans loved war.*

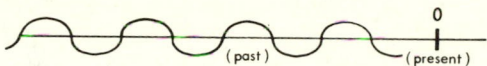

Il dînait à sept heures. *He used to have dinner at seven o'clock.*
Il allait souvent au théâtre. *He often went to the theatre.*
Quand il était à l'école, il n'étudiait pas assez. *When he was at school, he didn't study enough.*

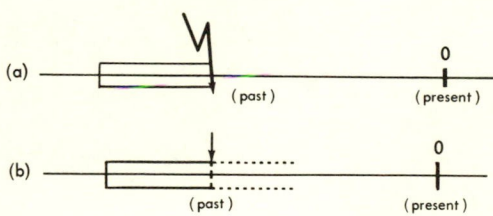

(*a*) **Il étudiait quand elle a téléphoné.** *He was studying when she called.*
(*b*) **A minuit il travaillait encore.** *At midnight he was still working.*
(*b*) **Quand je l'ai vu, il parlait à un groupe d'étudiants.** *When I saw him he was talking to a group of students.*

79

TABLE 8.1b

MAIN USES OF THE PASSÉ COMPOSÉ

OR PAST DEFINITE

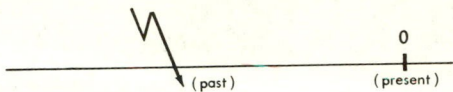

Il a frappé à la porte (il frappa . . .). *He knocked on the door.*
Il a acheté une maison (il acheta . . .). *He bought a house.*
Il est mort en 1940 (il mourut . . .). *He died in 1940.*

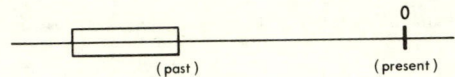

Ils ont parlé pendant deux heures (ils parlèrent . . .). *They spoke for two hours.*
Mon grand-père a travaillé toute sa vie (mon grand-père travailla . . .). *My grandfather worked all his life.*
Louis XIV a construit le palais de Versailles (Louis XIV construisit . . .). *Louis XIV built the palace of Versailles.*
L'empire romain a duré pendant plusieurs siècles (L'empire romain dura . . .). *The Roman Empire lasted for several centuries.*

🏮 CHAPTER IX 🏮

THE PAST OF THE PAST

Two tenses, the past perfect and past anterior, express actions that took place in the past *before* another past action.

A. THE PAST PERFECT

§9.2   The past perfect (*le plus-que-parfait*) is formed with the auxiliary in the imperfect plus the past participle of the verb. For instance:

j'avais acheté	*I had bought*	**nous avions acheté**
tu avais acheté		**vous aviez acheté**
il avait acheté		**ils avaient acheté**

MEANINGS AND TRANSLATIONS

§9.3   1. The past perfect is the basic tense used to express the past of the past. Usually it should be translated either by the past perfect or by the past tense.[1]

Il n'est pas venu à la soirée[2] et cependant je l'avais invité.	*He did not come to the party, and yet I had invited him.*
Avant de partir, il avait dit au revoir à ses amis.	*Before leaving he had said good-by to his friends.*

---

[1] English often uses two or more verbs in the past tense; French prefers to mark the difference between the first and subsequent actions.

[2] Note that **la soirée** means either *evening* or *party*, depending on context.

§9.4 2. After **si:** *if,* the past perfect is used to express imaginary actions or situations in the past which never materialized.

> **Si j'avais su!**   *If I had known!*
> **S'il avait étudié, il aurait moins de**   *If he had studied, he would have*
>   **difficultés.**[3]   *fewer difficulties.*

B. THE PAST ANTERIOR

§9.5 The past anterior (*le passé antérieur*) is formed with the auxiliary in the past definite plus the past participle of the verb. For example:

> **j'eus fini**   *I had finished*   **nous eûmes fini**
> **tu eus fini**   **vous eûtes fini**
> **il eut fini**   **ils eurent fini**

§9.6   MEANING AND TRANSLATION

Like the past perfect, the past anterior expresses actions accomplished before another past event took place. The past anterior, however, is literary and is found only in dependent clauses introduced by a conjunction of time, such as:

> **quand**   **dès que**[4]   **après que**   *after*
> **lorsque** } *when*   **aussitôt que** } *as soon as*   **à peine**   *hardly, no sooner*

Usually it should be translated by the past or past perfect.

> **Après qu'il eut remporté sa pre-**   *After he won his first victory, the*
>   **mière victoire, le général pour-**   *general pursued the enemies.*
>   **suivit les ennemis.**
> **A peine eut-il**[5] **fini son discours**   *No sooner had he finished his speech*
>   **qu'il partit.**   *than he left.*

---

[3] The past perfect is often used in coordination with the past of the conditional. (See §11.14.)

[4] Note that **dès** followed by a noun means *since* or *from.* For example: **dès le commencement:** *from the beginning.*

[5] An inversion is often used after **à peine.** This does not mean the sentence is interrogative. (See §14.5.)

C. WORDS USED TO EXPRESS
TIME AND DURATION

§9.7 *Pendant, durant*

These words can be used with verbs in any tense. They indicate the total duration of a period of time. Normally they should be translated by *during* or *for*.

Il a habité à Londres durant la guerre.	*He lived in London during the war.*
J'ai lu ce livre pendant le voyage.	*I read this book during the trip.*

Pendant is used with numerical expressions; it is often omitted when the period of time follows the verb.

Il a parlé (pendant) deux heures.	*He spoke (for) two hours.*

§9.8 *Il y a*

When **il y a** is used with an expression of time (in the past tense), it indicates how long ago an event took place; its normal translation is *ago*. Note the word order:

Il y a trois ans.	*Three years ago.*
Il y a longtemps.	*A long time ago.*
Ce temple a été construit il y a plus de deux mille ans.	*This temple was built over two thousand years ago.*

§9.9 *Auparavant*

This word, often accompanied by a verb in the past perfect, should be translated by *previously*.

Il a suivi des cours à Paris pendant un an. Auparavant il avait déjà étudié le français.	*He took courses in Paris for a year. Previously, he had already studied French.*

§9.10 *Depuis/il y a . . . que/voici . . . que* + *verb in the present tense*

These three constructions indicate that an action has started in the past and is still going on at the present moment. In the English translation, the present perfect should be used.

1. **Depuis** can be accompanied by words that indicate the chronological beginning of the action.[6]

---

[6] See §3.5.

Nous sommes ici depuis neuf heures et demie.   *We have been here since 9:30*

It can also be accompanied by words indicating the exact or approximate duration of the action, up to the present moment.

Il étudie le français depuis deux mois.   *He has been studying French for (the past) two months.*

Depuis quand êtes-vous ici? Je suis ici depuis dix minutes.   *How long have you been here? I've been here for ten minutes.*

J'attends depuis longtemps.   *I have been waiting for a long time.*

2. **Il y a** + expression of duration + **que** + verb in the present tense, also indicates that an action started in the past and is still going on at the present moment.

Il y a trois heures qu'il lit.   *He has been reading for three hours.*

This construction must not be confused with **il y a** plus verb in the past (see §9.8). Compare:

Il est allé à Paris il y a deux ans.   *He went to Paris two years ago.*

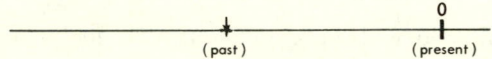

Il y a deux ans qu'il est à Paris.   *He has been in Paris for (the past) two years.*

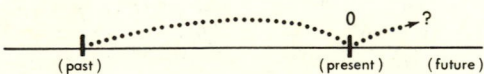

3. **Voici (voilà)** + expression of duration + **que** + verb in the present tense is also used to indicate that an action started in the past and is still going on.

Voici trois heures qu'il parle.   *He has been talking for three hours.*

Voilà longtemps que nous attendons.   *We have been waiting for a long time.*

§9.11 *Depuis/il y avait . . . que + verb in the imperfect*

These constructions indicate that an action started in the past and continued until a specific moment of the past. Normally a verb in the past perfect should be used in the English sentence.

Quand j'ai rencontré Paul, il habitait New York depuis 1960.   *When I met Paul, he had been living in New York since 1960.*

Il y avait trois heures que j'attendais quand le train est arrivé.   *I had been waiting for three hours when the train arrived.*

§9.12 ***Depuis/il y aura . . . que*** + *verb in the future*[7]

These expressions indicate that a future action will still be going on at a later date.

En l'an 3000 nous serons morts depuis longtemps (il y aura longtemps que nous serons morts). *In the year 3000 we will have been dead for a long time.*

§9.13 ***Aller/venir de*** (*in the imperfect*) + *infinitive*

These two expressions (cf. §3.9) indicate a near future or a recent past, in relation to a past moment.

J'allais sortir quand vous êtes arrivé. *I was about to leave when you arrived.*

Quand nous sommes arrivés au théâtre, la représentation venait de commencer. *When we arrived at the theater, the performance had just started.*

---

[7] See Chap. X.

CHAPTER X

A. THE FUTURE

§10.1   An action that is expected to take place in the near future can be expressed with **aller** in the present, plus the infinitive of the verb (see §3.9).

Nous allons lire ce livre.   *We're going to read this book.*

In conversational French, an action that seems imminent can be expressed with a verb in the present tense.

Je viens tout de suite.   *I'm coming right away.*

§10.2   THE FUTURE TENSE

Normally, an action which will take place in the future is expressed in the future tense. No auxiliary (such as *shall* or *will*) is used. The future tense is formed by adding to the infinitive of the verb the following endings:

FIRST GROUP		SECOND GROUP		THIRD GROUP	
marcher		finir		vendre	
je marcher	ai	je finir	ai	je vendr	ai
tu marcher	as	tu finir	as	tu vendr	as
il marcher	a	il finir	a	il vendr	a
nous marcher	ons	nous finir	ons	nous vendr	ons
vous marcher	ez	vous finir	ez	vous vendr	ez
ils marcher	ont	ils finir	ont	ils vendr	ont

1. The future endings of the three groups are identical.[1]

2. In the first and second groups, the verb contains the entire infinitive form before the ending.

3. Verbs of the third group ending in *-re* lose the *e* before the ending of the future is added.

4. A verbal form in which the entire infinitive appears is either a future or a present of the conditional (see §11.2).

§10.4   IRREGULAR FUTURES

INFINITIVE	IRREGULAR PART OF STEM	FUTURE TENSE	CONDITIONAL[2]
avoir *to have* savoir *to know*	-aur-	j'aurai je saurai	j'aurais je saurais
valoir *to be worth*[3]	-audr-	il vaudra	il vaudrait
faire *to do*	-fer-	je ferai	je ferais
tenir *to hold* venir *to come*	-iendr-[4]	je tiendrai je viendrai	je tiendrais je viendrais
vouloir *to want*	-oudr-	je voudrai	je voudrais
courir *to run* mourir *to die* pouvoir *to be able* voir *to see* envoyer *to send* acquérir *to acquire*	-rr-	je courrai je mourrai je pourrai je verrai j'enverrai j'acquerrai	je courrais je mourrais je pourrais je verrais j'enverrais j'acquerrais
apercevoir *to perceive* devoir *must* concevoir *to conceive* recevoir *to receive* pleuvoir *to rain*[5]	-vr-	j'apercevrai je devrai je concevrai je recevrai il pleuvra	j'apercevrais je devrais je concevrais je recevrais il pleuvrait

Two verbs have completely irregular stems:

---

[1] Notice the similarity between the endings of the future tense and the conjugation of **avoir** in the present. In Old French, the future was expressed with the infinitive of the verb followed by the present of **avoir.**

[2] See Chap. XI. Irregular verbs present the same irregularities in the future and in the conditional. But concentrate on the future tense for the moment.

[3] See §13.17.

[4] The following verbs are conjugated in the same way: **appartenir:** *to belong;* **détenir:** *to keep, to detain;* **maintenir:** *to maintain;* **obtenir:** *to obtain;* **provenir:** *to derive, to come from;* **retenir:** *to retain;* **revenir:** *to return;* **soutenir:** *to sustain;* **survenir:** *to occur.*

[5] See §13.17.

INFINITIVE	FUTURE TENSE	CONDITIONAL
être *to be*	je serai	je serais
	tu seras	tu serais
	il sera	il serait
	nous serons	nous serions
	vous serez	vous seriez
	ils seront	ils seraient
aller *to go*	j'irai	j'irais
	tu iras	tu irais
	il ira	il irait
	nous irons	nous irions
	vous irez	vous iriez
	ils iront	ils iraient

MEANINGS AND TRANSLATIONS

The future tense expresses:

§10.5   1. *Actions or situations that will take place in the future*. Normally it should be translated by the English future:

J'écrirai cette lettre demain.   *I'll write this letter tomorrow.*

§10.6   **NOTE**

After the conjunctions of time, French uses the future tense to express future actions. In this case, English uses the present. The most common conjunctions of time that can be followed by the future are:

quand	*when*	**dès que**	*as soon as*	**pendant que**	*while*
lorsque	*when*	**aussitôt que**	*as soon as*	**tandis que**	*while*
comme	*when, as*	**à mesure que**	*as, while*		

Je visiterai le Louvre quand j'irai à Paris.   *I'll visit the Louvre when I go to Paris.*

Téléphonez-moi dès que vous arriverez.   *Call me as soon as you arrive.*

Je vous aiderai aussitôt que je pourrai.   *I'll help you as soon as I can.*

§10.7   2. *Orders* (the future is more gentle than the imperative).

Vous porterez cette lettre à Monsieur Dupont.   *Take this letter to Mr. Dupont.*

§10.8   3. *The verbs* **avoir** *and* **être** *can express a probability or a possibility.*

Il n'est pas venu au bureau ce matin. Il sera malade.   *He did not come to the office this morning. He is probably (must be) sick.*

Le téléphone sonne. Ce sera Pierre.	*The telephone is ringing. It's probably (must be) Peter.*

B. THE FUTURE PERFECT

§10.9   The future perfect is formed with the auxiliary in the future and the past participle of the verb:

j'aurai fini	*I will have finished*	**nous aurons fini**
tu auras fini		**vous aurez fini**
il aura fini		**ils auront fini**

MEANINGS AND TRANSLATIONS

The future perfect expresses:

§10.10   1. *Actions that will take place in the future prior to a specific moment.* It should be translated by the English future perfect.

Il aura fini avant cinq heures.	*He will have finished before five o'clock.*
A la fin de la semaine, j'aurai lu les documents.	*By the end of the week, I will have read the documents.*

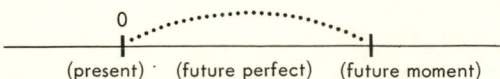

0   (present)   (future perfect)   (future moment)

§10.11   **NOTE**

After a conjunction of time (see §10.6), the French future perfect should be translated by a present perfect.

Je vous appellerai quand j'aurai fini.	*I'll call you when I have finished.*
Rendez-moi ces documents dès que vous les aurez lus.	*Return these documents to me as soon as you have read them.*

§10.12   2. *Actions that probably happened in the past.*

Il ne m'a pas écrit. Il aura perdu mon adresse.	*He hasn't written to me. He's probably lost my address.*

C. EXPRESSIONS OF
DURATION AND OF FUTURE ACTIONS

Dans + expression of time

This construction indicates the time when an action will take place. **Dans** should be translated by *in*.

Venez dans dix minutes.	*Come in ten minutes.*
Je serai libre dans une heure.	*I'll be free in an hour.*

En + expression of duration

This construction indicates the total duration of an action. It can be used with any tense.

Il a écrit la lettre en cinq minutes.	*He wrote the letter in five minutes (it took him five minutes).*
Les candidats devront répondre à ces questions en une heure.	*The candidates will have to answer these questions (with)in an hour.*

D'ici + expression of time

This construction indicates the period within which an action will take place. **D'ici** should be translated by *within*.

Vous recevrez une réponse d'ici dix jours.	*You will receive an answer within ten days.*

Pour + expression of duration

Normally **pendant** or **durant** are used to express a duration.[6] **Pour** indicates that the duration has changed or is subject to change.

Il était allé à Paris pour un an mais il y est resté dix ans.	*He went to Paris for a year, but (he) stayed for ten (years).*
Je pars en Europe pour deux mois.	*I'm planning to be (on being) in Europe for two months.*

Tout à l'heure

When used with a verb in the past, **tout à l'heure** indicates that the

---

[6] See §9.7. For example: **Je travaillerai pendant deux heures:** *I'll work for two hours* (definite period).

action took place recently; when used with the future, it indicates that the action will soon take place.

Il est venu tout à l'heure.	*He came a little while ago.*
Il viendra tout à l'heure.	*He'll come in a little while.*

Tout de suite

This expression indicates that an action takes place immediately; it can be used with a verb in any tense.

Il est venu tout de suite.	*He came right away.*
Venez tout de suite.	*Come right away.*

§10.14   EXPRESSIONS OF TIME

pendant	*during*	aujourd'hui	*today*
durant	*during*	maintenant	*now*
		à l'heure actuelle[9]	*right now, today*
comme	*as, while*	de nos jours	*nowadays*
au moment où	*as, while*	actuellement	*now, right now*
dès que	*as soon as*		
aussitôt que	*as soon as*	hier	*yesterday*
		demain	*tomorrow*
avant	*before*	la semaine dernière	*last week*
après	*after*	la semaine prochaine	*next week*
		d'aujourd'hui en huit	*a week from today*
tôt[7]	*early*		
tard	*late*		
en avance[8]	*early, ahead of time*	jusque	*until*
en retard	*late, tardy*	vers	*toward, around*

au dix-neuvième siècle	*in the nineteenth century*
au premier siècle de notre ère	*in the first century of the Christian era*
en 500 avant Jésus-Christ (av. J.-C.)	*in 500 B.C.*
au troisième millénaire avant Jésus-Christ	*in the third millennium before Christ*
du temps de Périclès	*in the days of Pericles*
à l'âge de la pierre	*in the Stone Age*
à l'époque glacière	*in the Ice Age*

---

[7] **Tôt** and **tard** refer to the time itself. For example: **Il est tôt:** *it's early;* **il est tard:** *it's late.*

[8] **En avance** and **en retard** refer to schedules. For example: **Il est en avance:** *he is early.*

[9] Note that **actuel** means *contemporary, present-day;* **actuellement:** *now, nowadays;* **les actualités:** *current events.* The French words for *actual* are: **réel, véritable.**

⟦ CHAPTER XI ⟧

A. THE CONDITIONAL

§11.1   The conditional expresses actions or situations which are possible but not certain. It has two tenses: present and past.

§11.2   THE PRESENT CONDITIONAL

No auxiliary (such as *should* or *would*) is used; the present conditional is formed by adding to the infinitive of the verb the following endings:

FIRST GROUP		SECOND GROUP		THIRD GROUP	
marcher		finir		vendre	
je marcher	ais	je finir	ais	je vendr	ais
tu marcher	ais	tu finir	ais	tu vendr	ais
il marcher	ait	il finir	ait	il vendr	ait
nous marcher	ions	nous finir	ions	nous vendr	ions
vous marcher	iez	vous finir	iez	vous vendr	iez
ils marcher	aient	ils finir	aient	ils vendr	aient

§11.3 <u>NOTE</u>

1. The endings of the three groups are identical.[1]

2. In the present conditional, a verb contains the entire infinitive (cf. §10.3).

---

[1] Note that the endings of the present conditional are the same as the endings of the imperfect. In the case of the imperfect they are added to the stem; in the present conditional they are added to the infinitive.

3. Verbs of the third group ending in *-re* lose the *e* before the conditional ending is added.

§11.4   IRREGULAR PRESENT CONDITIONALS

Irregular verbs present the same irregularities in the future and in the present conditional (see §10.4).

MEANINGS AND TRANSLATIONS
OF THE PRESENT CONDITIONAL

Usually the present conditional can be translated by the same tense in English. It expresses:

§11.5   1. *Polite requests.*

Pourriez-vous me dire où est la poste?	*Could you (would you be able to) tell me where the post office is?*

§11.6   2. *Hypothetical cases.*

On dit qu'il y aurait un trésor au fond du lac.	*People say (that) there might be a treasure at the bottom of the lake.*
Selon certains astronomes, la planète Vénus serait couverte de hautes montagnes.	*According to certain astronomers, the planet Venus may be covered with high mountains.*

§11.7   3. *Apprehension or indignation.*

Je condamnerais un innocent! Jamais!	*I would condemn an innocent person! Never!*

§11.8   4. *Wishes, desires, or advice.*

J'aimerais voyager.	*I'd like to travel.*
Vous devriez[2] lire ce livre.	*You should read this book.*

§11.9   5. *Actions that were considered future at a certain moment in the past.*

Je savais qu'il ferait cette faute.	*I knew that he would make this mistake.*
Il m'a dit qu'il viendrait le plus tôt possible.	*He told me that he would come as soon as possible.*

---

[2] The verb **devoir** will be studied more thoroughly in §14.7.

§11.10   6. *Actions that would materialize if the necessary condition were fulfilled.* The condition, when stated, is expressed in a clause beginning with **si:** *if,* and containing a verb in the imperfect (see §11.15).

A Paris, je parlerais français.	*In Paris I would speak French.*
Si j'étais riche, je voyagerais.	*If I were rich, I'd travel.*
Je lirais ce livre si j'avais le temps.	*I would read this book if I had time.*

§11.11   THE PAST CONDITIONAL

The past is formed with the present conditional of the auxiliary plus the past participle of the verb.

j'aurais vendu	*I would have sold*	**nous aurions vendu**
tu aurais vendu		**vous auriez vendu**
il aurait vendu		**ils auraient vendu**

MEANINGS AND TRANSLATIONS
OF THE PAST CONDITIONAL

The past conditional expresses:

§11.12   1. *Actions that may have taken place.*

Staline aurait été assassiné.	*Stalin may have been assassinated.*
L'accident aurait eu lieu vers minuit.	*The accident may have taken place around midnight.*

§11.13   2. *Plans and desires that never materialized.*

Napoléon aurait voulu envahir l'Angleterre.	*Napoleon would have liked to invade England.*
Cet étudiant aurait pu réussir mais il n'a même pas essayé.	*That student could have succeeded, but he didn't even try.*

§11.14   3. *Events that never materialized because the necessary condition was never fulfilled* (see §§9.4; 11.15).

Si j'avais eu assez d'argent, j'aurais fait un voyage.	*If I had had enough money, I would have taken a trip.*
S'il avait envoyé la lettre, je l'aurais reçue.	*If he had sent the letter, I would have received it.*
Si cet homme avait été vacciné, il ne serait pas mort.	*If that man had been vaccinated, he wouldn't have died.*

94

TABLE 11.1

CONDITION	CONCLUSION
si + VERB IN THE PRESENT INDICATIVE **s'il est malade** *if he is sick*	PRESENT INDICATIVE **c'est dommage** *it is a pity* IMPERATIVE **allez le voir** *go (and) see him* FUTURE **il restera chez lui** *he will stay home* PRESENT SUBJUNCTIVE **qu'il reste chez lui** *let him stay home*
si + VERB IN THE PASSÉ COMPOSÉ **s'il a perdu son livre** *if he has lost his book*	PRESENT INDICATIVE **c'est dommage** *it is a pity* IMPERATIVE **donnez-lui le vôtre** *give him yours* FUTURE **je lui prêterai le mien** *I will lend him mine* PRESENT SUBJUNCTIVE (see §12.7) **qu'il en achète un autre** *let him buy another one*
si + VERB IN THE IMPERFECT **s'il avait assez d'argent** *if he had enough money*	PRESENT CONDITIONAL **il voyagerait** *he would travel*
si + VERB IN THE PAST PERFECT **s'il avait eu assez d'argent** *if he had had enough money*	PRESENT CONDITIONAL **il serait ici** *he would be here* PAST CONDITIONAL **il aurait acheté une maison** *he would have bought a house*

Clauses beginning with **si** express a condition; they are usually in the present tense, the passé composé, the imperfect, or the past perfect (never in the conditional). They may be accompanied by a dependent clause that expresses the conclusion. Both clauses together form a coordinated structure, as shown in Table 11.1

B. DEMONSTRATIVE PRONOUNS

There are two kinds of demonstrative pronouns: variable and invariable.

§11.16   Vᴀʀɪᴀʙʟᴇ Dᴇᴍᴏɴsᴛʀᴀᴛɪᴠᴇ
Pʀᴏɴᴏᴜɴs

	SINGULAR		PLURAL	
M.	celui	this, that,	ceux	these, those,
F.	celle	the one	celles	the ones

§11.17   Mᴇᴀɴɪɴɢs ᴀɴᴅ Tʀᴀɴsʟᴀᴛɪᴏɴs

Celui, celle, ceux, celles + *-ci or -là*[3]

The translation should be *this one, that one, these, those*. When the pronoun is linked to the particle **-ci,** it refers to things that are close to the person speaking; when linked to **-là,** it refers to things further away.

Aimez-vous ces dessins? J'aime   *Do you like these drawings? I like*
celui-ci; je n'aime pas celui-là.   *this one; I don't like that one.*

Celui-ci, celui-là, etc. can refer to two different things or persons that

---

[3] The particles **-ci** and **-là** can be found after a noun. For example: **ce livre-ci:** *this book* (*right here*); **ce livre-là** *that book* (*over there*). **-Là** is also found in **jusque-là:** *as far as, up to, until then.*

have been mentioned in the preceding sentence. **Celui-ci** refers to the one mentioned last, *the latter;* **celui-là** refers to *the former.*

J'ai rencontré Pierre et son cousin. Celui-ci m'a parlé mais celui-là ne m'a rien dit.	*I met Peter and his cousin. The latter spoke to me, but the former didn't say anything to me.*

Celui, celle, ceux, celles + preposition

When followed by **de,** the demonstrative pronoun indicates origin or possession.[4]

Je n'ai pas mon livre, j'ai celui de mon frère.	*I don't have my book, I have my brother's.*
Les vins du Midi[5] sont plus doux que ceux de la Bourgogne.	*The wines from the South are sweeter than those from Burgundy.*
Regardez ces jolies maisons. J'aime surtout celle aux murs blancs.	*Look at those pretty houses. I especially like the one with the white walls.*

Celui, celle, ceux, celles + relative pronoun (qui, que, dont, où, lequel)

The usual translation is *the one, those,* etc.

Je dois acheter une autre auto; celle que j'ai est trop vieille.	*I must buy another car; the one I have is too old.*
J'ai quelques livres dans mon bureau; j'ai ceux dont j'ai constamment besoin.[6]	*I have a few books in my office; I have those that I need constantly.*
L'université a plusieurs télescopes. Voici celui avec lequel on observe la lune.	*The university has several telescopes. Here is the one with which we observe the moon.*
Ceux qui travaillent réussiront.[7]	*Those who work will succeed.*
On choisira ceux qui ont du talent.	*Those who are talented will be selected.[8]*

§11.18   INVARIABLE DEMONSTRATIVE
PRONOUNS

The invariable demonstrative pronouns are **ce** (**c'** + word beginning with a vowel): *this, that, he, she, it;* **ceci:** *this;* **cela** (**ça** in informal conversation): *that.*

---

[4] This construction is very common because French has no possessive case.

[5] Note that **midi** means *noon;* **le midi** means *(the) south;* **le Midi** means *the South (of France).*

[6] See §7.17.

[7] When the demonstrative pronoun does not refer to a noun previously mentioned, it always stands for a person.

[8] See §5.2.

1. *Ce precedes the third person (singular or plural) of the verb **être**.* Normally it should be translated by *it*.

ce + être +			
	adjective	c'est bon	*it (that) is good*
	adverb	c'est bien	*it (that) is fine*
	past participle	c'est fini	*it is finished*
	preposition	c'est pour vous	*it is for you*
	disjunctive pronoun	ce sont eux	*it is they*
	superlative	c'est le mieux	*it is the best*
	noun	c'est un chien	*it is a dog*
	proper name	c'est Paul	*it is Paul*
	adjective + à + infinitive	c'est facile à faire	*it is easy to do.*[9]

When **ce** refers to a person who has already been mentioned, it should be translated by *he* or *she*.

Qui est ce monsieur? C'est le directeur de l'usine.	*Who is that gentleman? He is the director of the plant.*
Je connais cette dame. C'est une amie de ma mère.	*I know that lady. She is a friend of my mother.*

2. ***Ce** + relative pronoun (**qui, que, dont, quoi**).* **Ce** precedes a relative pronoun when no antecedent is used. In this case, the relative pronoun refers to a general idea, not to a specific word, and **ce** is translated by *that* or *what*.

Je lis ce qui m'intéresse.	*I read what interests me.*[10]
Il fait ce qu'il veut.	*He does what he wants.*
Achetez ce dont vous avez besoin.	*Buy what you need.*
Je sais ce à quoi il pense.	*I know what he is thinking about.*
Ne croyez pas tout ce qu'on dit.	*Don't believe everything (that) people say.*

These pronouns refer to general ideas or to things that are not specifically designated. They can be translated by *this, that,* or *it*.

Ceci me surprend.	*It (that) surprises me (I am surprised).*
Cela arrive souvent.	*It (that) often happens.*
Prenez ceci, laissez cela.	*Take this; leave that.*

---

[9] Cf. **c'est facile à dire:** *it (that) is easy to say; easier said than done.*
[10] Cf. **je lis un livre qui m'intéresse:** *I am reading a book that interests me.*

Il a travaillé dans un hôpital; cela lui a donné une vaste expérience.[11]	*He's worked in a hospital; it's given him vast experience.*
Rappelez-vous de ceci:[12] cet homme n'est pas sincère.	*Remember this: that man is not sincere.*

In informal French, **cela** (or **ça**) can precede **ce:**

Cela, c'est incroyable!	That *is incredible!*

---

[11] See Chap. III, note 7.

[12] Generally, **ceci** announces that which follows; **cela** recalls what precedes.

▣ CHAPTER XII ▣

THE SUBJUNCTIVE

§12.1   The subjunctive mood expresses actions or situations that are doubtful or unlikely.[1] It has four tenses. Two of them, the present and past, are usual; the other two (see §§12.18-12.19) are literary and unusual in modern French.

§12.2   THE PRESENT SUBJUNCTIVE [2]

When a verb is in the subjunctive, it is usually preceded by **que**: *that*. To form the present of the subjunctive, the following endings are added to the stem:

FIRST GROUP		SECOND GROUP		THIRD GROUP	
marcher		**finir**		**vendre**	
que je march	e	que je fin	isse	que je vend	e
que tu march	es	que tu fin	isses	que tu vend	es
qu'il march	e	qu'il fin	isse	qu'il vend	e
que nous march	ions	que nous fin	issions	que nous vend	ions
que vous march	iez	que vous fin	issiez	que vous vend	iez
qu'ils march	ent	qu'ils fin	issent	qu'ils vend	ent

---

[1] French has three other moods: indicative, conditional, and imperative. The tenses of the indicative (present, passé composé, future, etc.) present objective and concrete actions or situations. The tenses of the conditional present that which is subject to a condition. The imperative conveys orders.

[2] The French subjunctive does not correspond to any specific tense or expression in English. (See §§12.4ff.)

Etre and **avoir** are highly irregular:

ÊTRE	AVOIR
que je sois	que j'aie
que tu sois	que tu aies
qu'il soit	qu'il ait
que nous soyons	que nous ayons
que vous soyez	que vous ayez
qu'ils soient	qu'ils aient

Three verbs have regular endings but highly irregular stems:

INFINITIVE	STEM	1 P. SG.
faire *to make*	fass-	que je fasse
pouvoir *to be able*	puiss-	que je puisse
savoir *to know*	sach-	que je sache

A certain number of verbs have regular endings but irregular stems in the three persons of the singular and the third person plural:

INFINITIVE	IRREGULAR PART OF STEM (*except* nous/vous)	1 P. SG.	1 P. PL.
aller *to go*	-aill-	que j'aille	que nous allions
prendre *to take*[3]	-enn-	que je prenne	que nous prenions
vouloir *to want*	-euill-	que je veuille	que nous voulions
mourir *to die*	-eur-	que je meure	que nous mourions
tenir *to hold*[4] venir *to come*[5]	-ienn-	que je tienne que je vienne	que nous tenions que nous venions
conquérir *to conquer*	-ier-	que je conquière	que nous conquérions
apercevoir[6] *to perceive* devoir *must* boire *to drink*[7]	-oiv-	que j'aperçoive que je doive que je boive	que nous apercevions que nous devions que nous buvions
voir *to see*[7]	-oi-	que je voie	que nous voyons

[3] Verbs conjugated like prendre are: apprendre, comprendre, entreprendre, reprendre, surprendre.

[4] Like tenir: appartenir, contenir, détenir, maintenir, retenir, soutenir.

[5] Like venir: devenir, parvenir, revenir, survenir.

[6] Like apercevoir: concevoir, décevoir, recevoir.

[7] **Boire** and **voir** are also irregular in the first and second persons of the plural: que nous buvions, que vous buviez; que nous voyons, que vous voyez.

Other verbs have regular endings but slightly irregular stems for all the persons of the present subjunctive. The same stem is found in the plural persons of the present indicative:

INFINITIVE	IRREGULAR PART OF STEM	3 P. PL. PRES. IND.	1 P. SG. PRES. SUBJ.
craindre *to fear*	-gn-[8]	ils craignent	que je craigne
joindre *to join*		ils joignent	que je joigne
plaindre *to pity*		ils plaignent	que je plaigne
vaincre *to vanquish*	-qu-	ils vainquent	que je vainque
dire *to tell*	-s-	ils disent	que je dise
lire *to read*		ils lisent	que je lise
plaire *to please*		ils plaisent	que je plaise
construire *to build* [9]		ils construisent	que je construise
coudre *to sew*		ils cousent	que je couse
croître *to grow*	-ss-	ils croissent	que je croisse
accroître *to increase*		ils accroissent	que j'accroisse
décroître *to decrease*		ils décroissent	que je décroisse
naître *to be born*		ils naissent	que je naisse
connaître *to know*		ils connaissent	que je connaisse
reconnaître *to recognize*		ils reconnaissent	que je reconnaisse
écrire *to write*	-v-	ils écrivent	que j'écrive
vivre *to live*		ils vivent	que je vive

§12.4 MEANINGS AND TRANSLATIONS
OF THE PRESENT SUBJUNCTIVE

The French subjunctive has no specific equivalent in English. The translation depends on the particular purpose of the subjunctive within the sentence.

PRELIMINARY REMARKS

1. The subjunctive is found almost exclusively in dependent clauses introduced by **qui** or **que**.[10]

2. The subjunctive has no future tense. The present tense is used to express both present and future actions.

---

[8] In the subjunctive, all verbs ending in **-indre** have **-gn-** in their stem.

[9] Like **construire: conduire, détruire, instruire, produire.**

[10] The use of the subjunctive in independent clauses is very limited (see §12.13).

Je suis content qu'il vienne aujourd'hui.	*I'm happy that he's coming today.*
Je suis content qu'il vienne demain.	*I'm happy that he'll come tomorrow.*

3. In all of the cases that we are about to see, the verb expresses an action that is, in one way or another, doubtful.

§12.5

The Present Subjunctive
in Dependent Clauses

The present subjunctive is found in the dependent clause when the main clause expresses:

§12.6   1. *Doubt or uncertainty.*

Je doute qu'il soit à la maison.	*I doubt that he's home.*
Je doute qu'il vienne demain.	*I doubt that he'll come tomorrow.*
Je ne suis pas sûr qu'il soit au bureau.	*I'm not sure that he's in the office.*

The idea of uncertainty is often expressed by an impersonal expression formed with the pronoun il:[11]

Il est possible qu'il soit malade.	*He may be sick.*

When the action seems certain or likely, the present or future indicative is used:

Je sais qu'il est à la maison.	*I know that he's home.*
Je suis certain qu'il viendra.	*I am certain that he'll come.*

§12.7   2. *A desire or an order.*

Je veux qu'il vienne immédiatement.	*I want him to come immediately.*
Le capitaine ordonne qu'on parte.	*The captain is ordering us to leave.*
Je voudrais que vous soyez poli.	*I'd like you to be polite.*
Je préfère qu'elle ne sache rien.	*I prefer that she know nothing.*

§12.8   3. *A necessity.*

Il faut que nous travaillions.	*We must work.*
Il est urgent qu'il vienne.	*It's urgent that he come.*
Il est nécessaire qu'il comprenne.	*He must understand.*

---

[11] Impersonal expressions will be studied in §13.17.

In the preceding cases (§§12.7-12.8), the subjunctive must be used in the dependent clause because there is always a possibility that the order will not be carried out or the necessary action will not be done.

§12.9   4. *An emotion or personal feeling.*

Je suis heureux que vous soyez ici.	*I'm glad that you're here.*[12]
Elle est en colère que vous partiez.	*She's angry that you're leaving.*
Il est surpris que nous sachions cela.	*He's surprised that we (should) know that.*
J'ai peur qu'il ne puisse pas venir demain.	*I'm afraid that he won't be able to come tomorrow.*
Qu'il soit content ou non, cela n'a aucune importance.	*Whether he's pleased or not makes no difference.*

§12.10   5. *A hypothesis* (not introduced by **si**).[13]

Supposons qu'il soit honnête.	*Let us suppose he's honest.*
Imaginons une ligne qui aille du pôle nord au pôle sud.	*Let us imagine a line going from the North Pole to the South Pole.*

§12.11

THE PRESENT SUBJUNCTIVE
IN ADJECTIVE CLAUSES

An adjective clause modifies the antecedent (i.e., the noun that precedes the relative pronoun). Usually the present subjunctive is used when the antecedent represents a person or a thing that:

1. *Does not exist.*

Il n'y a pas d'homme qui soit parfait.	*No man is perfect.*
Y a-t-il une ville en France qui soit plus belle que Paris?	*Is there a city in France (which is) more beautiful than Paris?*
Elle n'a pas trouvé de chapeau qui lui plaise.	*She hasn't found a hat (that) she likes.*

2. *May or may not exist.*

Je cherche un homme qui puisse m'aider.	*I'm looking for a man who can (might be able to) help me.*
On a besoin d'un officier qui sache le chinois.	*We need an officer who knows Chinese.*

---

[12] In this case, the action expressed in the dependent clause actually happened. The subjunctive mood is used, however, because it is presented in a personal or subjective way.

[13] For clauses beginning with **si**, see §11.15.

In such sentences, the use of the indicative or subjunctive is not determined by any formal grammar rule. The subjunctive suggests doubt; the indicative, certainty. In certain sentences, either an indicative or a subjunctive can be used, depending on the intention of the speaker. Let us compare:

Dans ce village y a-t-il un homme qui sache le chinois?	*In this village is there a man who knows (who happens to know) Chinese?*
Dans cette université y a-t-il un étudiant qui sait le chinois?	*In this university is there a student who knows Chinese?*

3. *Is modified by a superlative or by an expression of exclusiveness,* such as: **le seul:** *the only;* **l'unique:** *the unique;* **le premier:** *the first;* **le dernier:** *the last.*

La Cadillac est la meilleure auto que je connaisse.	*The Cadillac is the best car that I know of.*[14]
Le docteur Brun est le seul médecin qui puisse sauver ce malade.	*Doctor Brun is the only doctor who can save this patient.*
Le Louvre est le plus grand musée qui soit au monde.	*The Louvre is the largest museum in the world.*[15]

§12.12

THE PRESENT SUBJUNCTIVE
AFTER CERTAIN CONJUNCTIONS

The present subjunctive is used after:

1. *All conjunctions expressing a purpose.*

que	*that*	de façon que	*so that*	pour que	*so that*
afin que	*so that*	de façon à ce que	*so that*	de crainte que	*for fear lest*

Je parle lentement pour que vous compreniez.	*I am speaking slowly so that you may understand.*[16]

2. *Certain conjunctions of time.*

avant que *before*	**en attendant que** *until, before*	**jusqu'à ce que** *until*

Attendons jusqu'à ce qu'il revienne.	*Let's wait until he comes back.*

---

[14] In such sentences the subjunctive softens the statement and makes nuances (and loopholes!) possible.

[15] Usually the subjunctive is used after a superlative or an expression of exclusiveness even when the fact is considered certain.

[16] Cf. §§12.7-12.8. It is not certain that the purpose will be achieved.

3. *Certain conjunctions expressing a concession or restriction.*

bien que	*(even) though, in spite of the fact (that)*	**à moins que**	*unless*
quoique	*though, no matter what*	**sans que**	*without*

Il travaille bien qu'il soit fatigué.   *He works even though he is tired.*

4. *Certain literary expressions indicating an assumption or contrast.*

qui que	*no matter who, whoever*	**quoi que**	*no matter what*
quel [17] **que**	*no matter what, whatever*	**où que**	*wherever*

quelque + noun + **que** *whatever*
quelque + adj. + **que** ⎤
    si + adj. + **que** ⎦ *no matter how*

Qui que vous soyez, sauvez cet enfant.	*Whoever you may be, save this child.*
Quel que soit le résultat, écrivez-moi.	*Whatever the result may be, write to me.*
Quelles que soient les difficultés, je continuerai.	*No matter what the difficulties may be, I will continue.*
Quelque fort (si fort) qu'on soit, on doit se reposer.	*No matter how strong one may be, one has to rest.*
Quelques difficultés que nous ayons, nous devons continuer.	*Whatever difficulties we might have, we must continue.*

§12.13   # THE PRESENT SUBJUNCTIVE
IN INDEPENDENT CLAUSES

In independent clauses, the present subjunctive can express an order or an emotional reaction.

Qu'il parte!	*Let him go!*
Que Dieu vous entende!	*May God hear you!*

In a few idiomatic expressions, it is used without **que**.

Soit!	*So be it.*
Soit un triangle ABC.	*Given a triangle ABC.*
Vive le roi!	*Long live the king!*
Viennent les vacances!	*May the holidays come!*

---

[17] Note that **quel** must agree with the subject of the verb.

This tense is formed with the auxiliary in the present subjunctive plus the past participle of the verb.

que j'aie fini	que nous ayons fini
que tu aies fini	que vous ayez fini
qu'il ait fini	qu'ils aient fini

§12.15   MEANINGS OF THE
PAST SUBJUNCTIVE

The past subjunctive is always found in dependent clauses; like the present, it is used when the main clause expresses a doubt, order, necessity, emotion, etc. (see §§12.6-12.12).

§12.16   1. The past subjunctive indicates that the action took place (or may have taken place) before the action expressed in the main clause; [18] normally it should be translated by the English past tense:

Je suis heureux qu'il ait réussi.	*I am happy that he has succeeded.*
Il est possible qu'il soit déjà parti.	*He may have left already.*

When the main clause and the dependent clause express two past actions that both happened at the same time, French uses the present subjunctive while English uses a past tense:

Quand j'étais à l'hôpital, j'étais content que mon ami soit près de moi.	*When I was in the hospital, I was happy that my friend was with me.*

However, if the action of the dependent clause *preceded* the past action expressed in the main clause, the past subjunctive is used. In this case, a past perfect should be used in English.

Il était en colère que j'aie fini avant lui.	*He was angry that I had finished before he did (before him).*

§12.17   2. The past subjunctive indicates that an action might happen at a future moment, prior to a certain deadline. In this case, it is similar to the future perfect (see §10.10), but of course it presents the action with a halo of doubt. The English present perfect should be used.

---

[18] In the case of the subjunctive mood, the word *past* does not have an absolute, but a relative meaning. The dependent clause should always be considered in relation to the main clause.

Il faut que j'aie fini avant la fin de la semaine.	*I will have to have finished before the end of the week.*
Le professeur voudrait que les étudiants aient lu ce livre avant l'examen.	*The teacher would like the students to have read this book before the exam.*

§12.18   * THE IMPERFECT SUBJUNCTIVE

This tense is highly literary; nowadays it is almost always replaced by the present subjunctive. It is sufficient to be able to recognize the third person singular, and plural.

FIRST GROUP	SECOND GROUP	THIRD GROUP
marcher	finir	vendre
qu'il marchât	qu'il finît	qu'il vendît
qu'ils marchassent	qu'ils finissent	qu'ils vendissent

ÊTRE	AVOIR
qu'il fût	qu'il eût
qu'ils fussent	qu'ils eussent

The imperfect subjunctive is found in dependent clauses and is always accompanied by a main clause in a past tense.

Le roi marchait lentement afin que tout le monde le vît.	*The king was walking slowly so that everyone would see him.*

§12.19   * THE PAST PERFECT SUBJUNCTIVE

This tense is also literary and today is almost always replaced by the past subjunctive. It is formed with the auxiliary in the imperfect subjunctive plus the past participle of the verb. For instance: **qu'il eût fait, qu'ils eussent fait.**

The past perfect subjunctive is found in dependent clauses that are accompanied by a main clause in a past tense. It indicates that the action expressed in the dependent clause took place before that expressed in the main clause.

---

* The material in §§12.18-12.19 is not so very common that a beginner needs to study them in depth. To translate literary texts, it is sufficient to be able to recognize the third person, singular or plural.

| Le roi se réjouit que ses ennemis eussent capitulé. | *The king rejoiced that his enemies had capitulated.* |

The past perfect subjunctive can also be used instead of the past conditional (see §11.14) to express past events that never materialized because the necessary condition was not fulfilled:

| Si le général avait été battu, il eût été banni. | *If the general had been defeated, he would have been banished.* |

In highly literary French, the past perfect subjunctive can also be used instead of the past perfect indicative to express past conditions that were never fulfilled.

| Si le général eût été battu, il eût été banni. | *If the general had been defeated, he would have been banished.* |

§12.20   SUBJUNCTIVE OR INDICATIVE?

SPECIAL CASES

As a whole, the subjunctive expresses actions or situations that seem doubtful or nonexistent. A few verbs, however, must be studied separately.

Douter: *to doubt.* This verb is always accompanied by a dependent clause in the subjunctive—even when it is negative.

| Je doute qu'il soit malade. | *I doubt that he is sick.* |
| Je ne doute pas qu'il soit honnête; cependant je ne veux pas prendre de risques. | *I don't doubt that he is honest; however I don't want to take any chances.* |

To sound more categorical, one would say:

| Je sais (je suis sûr) qu'il est honnête. | *I know (I am sure) he is honest.* |

Se douter: *to suspect.*[19] Here the subject is almost positive about what he says, so the verb is accompanied by a dependent clause in the indicative.

| Je me doute qu'il sera en retard. | *I suspect he will be late.* |
| Le policier s'est douté[20] que l'assassin était caché dans la forêt. | *The policeman suspected that the murderer was hidden in the forest.* |

Espérer: *to hope.* This verb is always accompanied by a verb in the

---

[19] Note that **douter** and **se douter** differ greatly in meaning (see §6.5).
[20] See §8.15.

indicative. Of course the subject cannot be sure that his hope will be fulfilled, but he believes (or wants to believe) that it can be.

J'espère qu'il a réussi.	*I hope he has succeeded.*
Il espère qu'elle viendra demain.	*He hopes she will come tomorrow.*

Nier: *to deny.* Normally this verb is accompanied by a dependent clause in the subjunctive.

Il nie que j'aie dit cela.	*He denies that I said that.*
Je ne nie pas qu'il ait fait des progrès.	*I don't deny that he has progressed.*

Penser: *to think;* **croire:** *to believe.* When these verbs are in the affirmative, they are accompanied by a dependent clause in the indicative.

Il croit qu'il n'y a plus de danger.	*He believes (that) there is no more danger.*
Je pense qu'il viendra demain.	*I think (that) he will come tomorrow.*

When **penser** and **croire** are in the interrogative or negative, they are accompanied by a dependent clause in the subjunctive:

Croyez-vous qu'il soit malade?	*Do you think he is sick?*
Je ne pense pas[21] **que la situation soit très grave.**	*I don't think the situation is very serious.*

---

[21] To be more categorical one would have to say: **Je sais (je crois, je pense) que la situation n'est pas très grave.**

🖿 CHAPTER XIII 🖾

A. THE INFINITIVE

§13.1   The infinitive is invariable and is characterized by the following endings:

First group: **-er**   Second group: **-ir**   Third group: **-re**

§13.2   THE INFINITIVE AS A NOUN

Certain infinitives can be used as nouns: **le pouvoir:** *the power;* **le devoir:** *duty;* **le rire:** *laughter.*

Vouloir, c'est pouvoir.	*Where there's a will there's a way.*
Jean-Paul Sartre a écrit *L'Etre et le néant.*	*Jean-Paul Sartre wrote* Being and Nothingness.

§13.3   THE INFINITIVE
                    AS THE OBJECT OF A VERB

The infinitive can be used directly (i.e., without a preposition) or indirectly. Since it has no subject of its own, it is understood that the action expressed by the infinitive is done by the subject of the conjugated verb.

1. *The infinitive is used directly after verbs expressing an opinion, a desire, or a movement.*

Je veux partir.	*I want to leave.*
Il aime lire.	*He likes to read.*

111

| Elle préfère rester ici. | She prefers to stay here. |
| Il vient manger. | He is coming to eat. |

If the second verb needs a different subject, it must constitute a different clause. Let us compare:

J'espère aller à Paris.	I hope to go to Paris.
J'espère que Paul ira à Paris.	I hope Paul will go to Paris.
Je veux partir.	I want to leave.
Je veux qu'il parte.	I want him to leave.
Il préfère rester.	He prefers to stay.
Il préfère que nous restions.	He prefers that we stay.

2. *The infinitive is used after the preposition à or de.* The preposition plus the infinitive should be translated by the English infinitive.

Il hésite à venir.	He hesitates to come.
Je commence à comprendre.	I'm beginning to understand.
Il a décidé de partir.	He has decided to leave.
Je jure de dire la vérité.	I swear to tell the truth.
Il refuse de signer.	He refuses to sign.
Il demande à mon ami de l'aider.	He is asking my friend to help him.

§13.4   SPECIAL CONSTRUCTIONS

1. *With verbs of perception.* Following verbs such as **apercevoir:** *to perceive;* **écouter:** *to listen;* **entendre:** *to hear;* **regarder:** *to look at;* **sentir:** *to feel, to smell;* and **voir:** *to see,* the infinitive is used directly. However, the subject of the conjugated verb does not do the action expressed by the infinitive.

J'entends chanter les oiseaux. ⎱	
J'entends les oiseaux chanter. ⎰	I hear the birds sing.
Je les entends chanter.	I hear them sing.
J'ai vu partir le bateau. ⎱	
J'ai vu le bateau partir. ⎰	I saw the boat leave.
Je l'ai vu partir.	I saw it leave.
Il a senti venir l'orage. ⎱	
Il a senti l'orage venir. ⎰	He felt the storm coming.
Il l'a senti venir.	He felt it coming.

§13.5   2. *With the verb faire: to make, to do.* When this verb is followed by an infinitive, its subject is the cause of the action, not the agent. Usually this idea is expressed in English by *to have* or *to make* plus the past participle.

| Il fait construire une maison. | He is having a house built. |
| Je fais réparer mon auto. | I'm having my car repaired. |

Je la fais réparer.	*I'm having it repaired.*
L'infirmière fait bouillir[1] l'eau.	*The nurse is boiling the water.*
Jeanne se fait faire une robe.	*Jeanne is having a dress made (for herself).*

The name of the agent can accompany the infinitive.

Le directeur fait travailler les employés.	*The director is making the employees work.*
Le directeur les fait travailler.	*The director is making them work.*
Le professeur fait traduire les étudiants.	*The teacher is making the students translate.*
Le professeur les fait traduire.	*The teacher is making them translate.*

When the infinitive has a direct object, the name of the agent is preceded by a preposition: **par:** *by* or **à:** *to.*

Le patron fait écrire la lettre par la secrétaire.[2]	*The boss is making the secretary write the letter.*
Le patron la[3] fait écrire par la secrétaire.	*The boss is making the secretary write it.*
Le patron la lui fait écrire.	*The boss is making her write it.*

The preceding examples show that when the infinitive is accompanied by a single object, it is a direct object. But when there are two objects, the direct object expresses the thing being done and the indirect object, the agent.

§13.6   3. *With the verb **laisser**: to let, to leave, to allow.* With this verb plus the infinitive, the subject *allows* the action to be done.

Je laisse parler les gens.[4]	*I let people talk.*
Je les laisse parler.	*I let them talk.*
Laissez passer les autos.	*Let the cars go through.*
Laissez-les passer.	*Let them go through.*

The infinitive can be accompanied by two nouns: one represents the agent and the other, the thing done.

Le professeur laisse l'étudiant finir l'expérience.	*The teacher is letting the student finish the experiment.*
Le docteur laisse l'infirmière faire cette opération.	*The doctor is letting the nurse perform this operation.*
Le docteur la[5] laisse faire cette opération.	*The doctor is letting her perform this operation.*

---

[1] Note that **bouillir** is irregular: **l'eau boue:** *the water is boiling.*
[2] If **la secrétaire** were the only object, the sentence would be: **le patron fait écrire la secrétaire:** *the boss is making the secretary write.*
[3] Note that **la** here stands for the letter.
[4] Note that **les gens:** *people* is always plural; **le peuple** means *working class,* **les peuples** means *peoples, nations.*
[5] Here **la** stands for the nurse.

Le docteur la[6] laisse faire par l'infirmière.	*The doctor is letting the nurse do it.*
Le docteur la lui[7] laisse faire.	*The doctor is letting her do it.*

COMMON EXPRESSIONS

1. The construction **faire** + infinitive is very common. Let us note:

faire apprendre	*to make someone learn, to teach*
faire comprendre	*to make someone understand, to explain*
faire entrer	*to let in, to invite in*
faire savoir	*to inform, to announce*
faire venir	*to call, to bid, to order from*
faire visiter	*to show around*
faire voir	*to show, to demonstrate, to prove*

2. Also very common is **savoir** + infinitive, meaning *to know how.*

Il sait lire.	*He knows how to read.*
Savez-vous danser?	*Do you know how to dance?*
Mon grand-père savait parler le russe.	*My grandfather knew how to speak Russian.*

3. A verb of movement followed by an infinitive usually expresses a purpose. In the English translation, the word *and* or a special construction should often be used.

Il va voir son ami.	*He's going to see his friend.*
Venez m'aider.	*Come (and) help me.*
Il va chercher le docteur.	*He's going for the doctor.*
J'ai envoyé chercher les documents.	*I've sent for the documents.*

THE INFINITIVE AFTER PREPOSITIONS

In French, when a verb follows a preposition (except **en**), it is always in the infinitive (see §13.11). In English, some prepositions are followed by the infinitive, others by the present participle.

Il est parti sans dire au revoir.	*He left without saying good-by.*
Vous êtes ici pour travailler.	*You are here (in order) to work.*
Il est allé à la poste après avoir écrit la lettre.	*He went to the post office after having written the letter.*
J'ai étudié l'espagnol avant d'étudier le français.	*I studied Spanish before studying French.*

---

[6] Here **la** stands for the operation.

[7] **La:** the operation; **lui:** the nurse. Note that when **laisser** + infinitive is accompanied by two object pronouns, the indirect object pronoun always represents the agent. Cf. §13.5.

B. THE PRESENT PARTICIPLE

§13.9   The present participle is invariable. It is characterized by the ending **-ant**: *-ing*.

FIRST GROUP	SECOND GROUP	THIRD GROUP
marcher	finir	vendre
marchant	finissant[8]	vendant

§13.10   Irregular Present Participles

In the present participle, the stem of certain verbs is somewhat irregular:

INFINITIVE	IRREGULAR PART OF STEM	PRESENT PARTICIPLE[9]
avoir *to have*	ay-	ayant
savoir *to know*	-ch-	sachant
craindre *to fear*	-gn-[10]	craignant
prendre *to take*[11]	-n-	prenant
vaincre *to vanquish*	-qu-	vainquant
dire *to say*		disant
lire *to read*		lisant
faire *to make*	-s-	faisant
plaire *to please*		plaisant
construire *to build*[12]		construisant
coudre *to sew*		cousant
croître *to grow*[13]		croissant
naître *to be born*	-ss-	naissant
connaître *to know*		connaissant
paraître *to appear, to seem*		paraissant
boire *to drink*	-v-	buvant
écrire *to write*		écrivant
voir *to see*	-y-	voyant
croire *to believe*		croyant

---

[8] Note the particle **iss** characteristic of the second group.

[9] Most of the irregularities found in the present participle are similar to those found in the third person plural indicative and in the subjunctive. Cf. §12.3.

[10] Like **craindre** are conjugated all the verbs in **-indre**.

[11] Like **prendre**: apprendre, comprendre, entreprendre, reprendre, surprendre.

[12] Like **construire**: conduire, détruire, instruire, produire.

[13] Like **croître**: accroître, décroître.

The present participle has no subject of its own. It is understood that the action expressed by the present participle is done by the subject of the conjugated verb of the clause.

Il lit en marchant.	*He reads while walking (as he walks).*

Two cases can be found:

1. *The two actions are parallel in time.*

Il a monté l'escalier en courant.	*He ran up the stairs* (lit., *he climbed the stairs running*).
Je lirai en attendant le train.	*I'll read while waiting for the train.*

Simultaneity can also be stressed with the word **tout**. This construction is often used when the two actions seem to be in contradiction. **Tout** can be translated by (*even*) *while* or (*even*) *though*.

Il fume tout en conduisant.	*He smokes (even) while driving.*
Il est sorti tout en étant malade.	*He went out (even) though he was sick.*

2. *The present participle expresses the cause of the action or the way in which it was done.* Here, *by* or *as* should be used in English.

On apprend à conduire en conduisant.	*You learn how to drive by driving.*
Je suis tombé en montant l'escalier.	*I fell (as I was) going up the stairs.*
Le docteur a sauvé ce malade en lui donnant une transfusion de sang.	*The doctor saved this patient by giving him a blood transfusion.*

The Present Participle
Without En

Three cases can be found:

1. The two actions take place at the same time but are not done by the same agent.

Je l'ai vu traversant la rue.	*I saw him crossing the street.*
Nous avons entendu une femme criant au secours.	*We heard a woman calling for help.*

2. The two actions are accomplished by the same agent, but the action expressed by the verb in the present participle precedes the other action.

Prenant son chapeau, il est sorti.	*He took his hat and left.*

3. The verb in the present participle expresses a general cause. Normally, *since* should be used in English.

Etant infirme, il ne peut pas vo- **yager.**	*Since he's crippled, he can't travel.*

§13.13   ADJECTIVES IN -ANT

Like all adjectives, they agree with the noun they qualify.

un livre intéressant	*an interesting book*
une pièce amusante	*an amusing play*
une expression courante	*a common expression*
un travail fatigant	*a tiresome work*

C. THE PASSIVE VOICE

§13.14   When a sentence is in the passive voice, the subject does not accomplish the action; it remains passive. Let us compare:

Le cuisinier fait les gâteaux.	*The cook makes the cakes.* (ACTIVE)
Les gâteaux sont faits par le cuisinier.	*The cakes are made by the cook.* (PASSIVE)

§13.15   FORMS

In French, as in English, the passive is formed by **être:** *to be* followed by the past participle.

Le bâtiment (la maison) est construit(e)	*(is built)*
a été construit(e)	*(has been, was built)*
était construit(e)	*(was being built)*
avait été construit(e)	*(had been built)*
sera construit(e)	*(will be built)*
serait construit(e)	*(would be built)*
aurait été construit(e)	*(would have been built)*
Il faut que . . . soit construit(e)	*(has to be built)*
Il (elle) doit être construit(e)	*(has to be built)*

§13.16   **NOTE**

This construction presents a certain difficulty for the beginner because of the intransitive verbs that use the auxiliary **être** to form their compound tenses.[14] The following points should be remembered:

1. The intransitive verbs conjugated with **être** can *never* have a direct object. Compare:

La lettre est signée.	*The letter is signed.* (PASSIVE)
Il est parti.	*He has left.* (INTRANS.)
L'expérience est terminée.	*The experiment is finished.* (PASSIVE)
Mon ami est arrivé.	*My friend has arrived.*[15] (INTRANS.)

2. A verb in the passive can always be turned into the active voice and be used with a direct object.

Le travail est fini.	*The work is finished.* (PASSIVE)
L'homme finit le travail.	*The man is finishing the work.* (ACTIVE)

D. IMPERSONAL VERBS AND EXPRESSIONS

§13.17   All impersonal verbs are accompanied by the subject pronoun **il**: *it*. They express the following concepts:

The time

Il est dix heures.	*It is ten o'clock.*
Il est six heures du soir.	*It is six p.m.*
Il est minuit.[16]	*It is midnight.*
Il est tôt.	*It's early.*
Il est tard.	*It's late.*
Il est midi.	*It's noon.*

The weather

Il fait froid.[17]	*It's cold.*
Il fait chaud.	*It's hot.*
Il pleut.	*It's raining.*
Il neige.	*It's snowing.*
Il fait du soleil.	*It's sunny.*

---

[14] See §8.16.

[15] We could say: **il signe la lettre, il termine l'expérience.** On the other hand, **partir** and **arriver** cannot have a direct object. Thus when intransitive verbs are accompanied by **être,** they are in a compound tense; when all other verbs are accompanied by **être,** they are in the passive voice.

[16] See Chap. IV, note 2.

[17] Note the use of **faire** to describe the weather.

Il fait du vent.	*It's windy.*
Il fait beau.	*The weather's fine.*
Il fait nuit.	*It's dark.*

An obligation[18]

Il faut.	*It is necessary.*
Il est nécessaire.	*It is necessary.*
Il importe.	*It is necessary.*
Il convient.	*It is advisable, necessary.*
Il est impérieux.	*It is imperative.*
Il est urgent.	*It is urgent.*
Il est indispensable.	*It is indispensable.*
Il est inévitable.	*It is inevitable, unavoidable.*
Il est préférable.	*It is preferable.*
Il vaut mieux.[19]	*It is preferable, better.*

A possibility

Il est vrai.	*It is true.*
Il est probable.	*It is probable.*
Il est possible.	*It is possible.*
Il est vraisemblable.	*It is likely.*
Il est évident.	*It is obvious.*
Il semble que.	*It seems that.*
Il se peut que.	*It may be that.*
Il est improbable.	*It is unlikely.*
Il est douteux.	*It is doubtful.*
Il est impossible.	*It is impossible.*
Il y a une chance sur dix.	*There is one chance in ten.*

A frequency

Il est fréquent.	*It is frequent.*
Il est habituel.	*It is usual.*
Il est normal.	*It is normal.*
Il est courant.	*It is common.*
Il existe.	*There is, there are.*
Il arrive que.	*It happens that.*
Il est exceptionnel que.	*It is unusual that.*
Il est rare que.	*It seldom happens that, it is rare that.*

§13.18 *Other impersonal expressions*

Il y a: *there is, there are* (see §1.8).

Il y aura un examen.	*There will be an exam.*
Il y a eu un accident.	*There was an accident.*

---

[18] These expressions can be followed by an infinitive or a subjunctive. Compare: **il faut travailler:** *it is necessary to work* and **il faut qu'il travaille:** *it is necessary for him to work (he has to work).*

[19] This expression (from **valoir:** *to be worth*) is very common. It is often used in the conditional: **il vaudrait mieux:** *it would be better.*

Il suffit: *it is sufficient, it is enough.*

Pour passer cet examen, il suffit d'étudier pendant un mois.	*To pass this exam, it is (will be) sufficient to study for a month.*

Il manque: *(something) is missing.*

Il manque de l'argent.	*Some money is missing.*

Il reste: *(something) is left.*

Il reste de l'eau au fond du tube.	*Some water is left at the bottom of the tube.*
Il me reste dix dollars.	*I have ten dollars left.*

Il se trouve que: *it so happens that.*

Il se trouve que je ne serai pas libre demain.	*It so happens I won't be free tomorrow.*

Il s'agit de + infinitive: *it is necessary, one must, one has to.*

Maintenant il s'agit de travailler.	*Now we have to work.*

Il s'agit de + noun: *it is a question of, it is a matter of.*

Dans ce chapitre il s'agit des causes de la chute de l'Empire romain.	*This chapter deals with the causes of the fall of the Roman Empire.*
Il s'agit d'un cas d'anémie.	*This is a case of anemia.*
De quoi s'agit-il?	*What is the matter?*

Il est + adjective + **de** + infinitive: *it is.*

Il est agréable de faire un voyage.	*It is pleasant to take a trip.*

Il est: *there is, there are.* This construction is sometimes used in literary French in place of **il y a.**

Il est des pays où il ne pleut jamais.	*There are countries where it never rains.*

⫾ CHAPTER XIV ⫾

This chapter contains no new basic grammar. It is designed primarily for students who are beginning to read literary or scholarly French.

A. ADJECTIVES WITH TWO SHADES OF MEANING

A few adjectives differ in meaning according to whether they precede or follow the noun that they qualify. The most common of these are:

	BEFORE NOUN	AFTER NOUN
ancien	*former* **mon ancienne adresse** *my former address*	*ancient, old* **un livre ancien** *an ancient book*
brave	*kind, good* **un brave homme** *a kind man*	*brave* **un soldat brave** *a brave soldier*
certain	*faint, indefinite, indeterminate* **un certain sourire** *a vague smile*	*positive, certain* **un résultat certain** *a positive result*
dernier	*last (of a series)* **le dernier jour** *the last day*	*last, preceding* **la semaine dernière** *last week*
divers	*several, diverse* **diverses personnes** *several persons*	*diversified, varied* **des exemples divers** *various (kinds of) examples*

gentil	noble	nice, sweet
	un gentilhomme[1]	**un enfant gentil**
	a nobleman	*a nice child*
grand	great	tall
	un grand homme	**un homme grand**
	a great man	*a tall man*
mauvais	wrong	bad, wicked
	une mauvaise décision	**un homme mauvais**
	a wrong decision	*a wicked man*
même[2]	same	very
	la même réponse	**la réponse même**
	the same answer	*the very answer*
pauvre	poor, to be pitied [3]	poor, destitute
	le pauvre homme	**un homme pauvre**
	the poor fellow	*a poor man*
propre	own, personal	clean
	ma propre maison	**un costume propre**
	my own house	*a clean suit*
sale	nasty, unpleasant	dirty
	une sale situation	**des mains sales**
	a nasty situation	*dirty hands*
seul	only, single, mere	alone, solitary
	un seul homme	**un homme seul**
	one single man	*a solitary man*
simple	simple, mere	simple, plain
	un simple mot	**une décoration simple**
	a mere word	*a simple decoration*
vrai	real	true
	une vraie tragédie	**une histoire vraie**
	a real tragedy	*a true story*

B.   GEOGRAPHICAL NAMES

§14.2   CONTINENTS, COUNTRIES,
                              PROVINCES

Names of continents, countries, and provinces have both gender and

---

[1] Note that this is one word; it is used historically only.
[2] For the conjunction **même** see §14.8.
[3] The use of **pauvre** before the noun **homme** is often sarcastic.

number. The gender of most countries stems from mythological or historical factors. Most European countries have feminine names with an *e* ending. Usually the gender of more recent geographical terms has been determined by the sound (**la Virginie, le Texas, le Chili**).

L'Italie est belle.	*Italy is beautiful.*
L'Amérique du Sud est fascinante.	*South America is fascinating.*
La Normandie est une vieille province.	*Normandy is an old province.*
J'aime le Canada.	*I like Canada.*

Masculine and plural names are *always* preceded by the article, with which, following the normal rules, the prepositions **à** and **de** contract.

Mes amis sont au Japon.	*My friends are in Japan.*
La richesse des Etats-Unis.	*The wealth of the United States.*
Ce vin vient du Portugal.	*This wine comes from Portugal.*

Feminine names are preceded by the definite article except when they follow **en** or **de**.

Il est en Espagne.	*He is in Spain.*
Nous irons en Suisse.	*We will go to Switzerland.*
Cette compagnie exporte en Australie.	*This company exports to Australia.*
Il vient de Suède.	*He comes from Sweden.*

When **de** does not indicate origin, however, the article is kept.

Nous parlons de la France.	*We are talking about France*
La civilisation de la Grèce.	*The civilization of Greece.*

NOTE

La France du nord.	*Northern France.*
Le nord de la France.	*The north of France.*
L'Amérique centrale.	*Central America.*
Le centre de l'Espagne.	*The central part of Spain.*

§14.3   CITIES

Names of cities are preceded by an article only when they are modified by an adjective:

Il habite à Paris.	*He lives in Paris.*
Ils vont à Rome.	*They are going to Rome.*
La Rome antique.	*Ancient Rome.*

However, the names of a few cities always contain an article. For example: **Le Havre, Le Mans, La Nouvelle Orléans** (*New Orleans*), **Le**

Caire (*Cairo*). When they are preceded by **à** or **de,** the usual contractions occur.

Il va au Havre.	*He is going to Le Havre.*
Les courses du Mans.	*The races of Le Mans.*

§14.4 RIVERS

Names of rivers are either masculine or feminine. Their "personality" usually explains their gender.

La Seine est une rivière paisible.	*The Seine is a peaceful river.*
Le Rhône est violent.	*The Rhone is violent.*

§14.5

C. INVERSIONS IN NONINTERROGATIVE SENTENCES

Normally the subject follows the verb when a sentence is interrogative. However, in literary French the subject is often placed after the verb in the following instances:

1. *After a quotation.*

Je suis prêt, dit-il.	*I'm ready, he said.*
Je ne le ferai pas, répondit-il.	*I won't do it, he answered.*

2. *In exclamatory sentences.*

Puisse-t-il réussir!	*May he succeed!*
Vive le roi!	*Long live the king!*

3. *In literary sentences beginning with an adjective.*

Rares sont les hommes honnêtes!	*Few are the honest men!*
Profond était le silence!	*Profound was the silence!*

4. *In literary sentences which begin with:* **à peine:** *hardly;* **ainsi:** *thus;* **aussi** (or **si**): *so, therefore;* **au moins:** *at least;* **du moins:** *at least;* **encore:** *still, yet;* **en vain:** *in vain;* **rarement:** *seldom;* **peut-être:** *perhaps;* **probablement:** *probably;* **sans doute:** *doubtless;* **toujours:** *yet, nevertheless;* **jamais:** *never.*

A peine a-t-il dit un mot.	*He hardly said a word.*
Aussi décida-t-il de partir.	*So he decided to leave.*

Ainsi parla le roi.
Peut-être Paul se trompe-t-il.

Thus spoke the king.
Maybe Paul is making a mistake.

D. THE USE OF NE IN
NONNEGATIVE SENTENCES

Ne constitutes the first part of all negative forms.[4] In literary French, it is sometimes the only word indicating the negation.[5]

However, **ne** can also be found in literary sentences that are not negative at all, and where it has no real meaning. This superfluous (or pleonastic) **ne** can be found only in a few specific cases:[6]

1. *With verbs and expressions indicating fear:* **craindre:** *to fear;* **avoir peur:** *to be afraid;* **de crainte que, de peur que:** *for fear that, lest.*

J'ai peur qu'il (ne) soit malade.[7]

I'm afraid that he's sick (that he will be sick).

2. *With the following verbs indicating avoidance or prevention:* **empêcher:** *to prevent;* **éviter:** *to avoid;* **prendre garde:** *to watch out.*

Empêchons que cette catastrophe (n')arrive.
Evitez que la montre (ne) tombe.

Let us prevent this catastrophe from happening.
See that the watch does not fall.

3. *After the following expressions:* **à moins que:** *unless* and **avant que:** *before.*[8]

Restez au bureau à moins que je (ne) vous appelle.
Il est mort avant que le docteur (ne) puisse arriver.

Stay in the office unless I call you.
He died before the doctor could arrive.

4. *After the following expressions of concession:* **ne pas nier:** *not to deny* and **ne pas douter:** *not to doubt.*

Je ne nie pas qu'il (ne) soit malheureux, mais néanmoins il est coupable.

I don't deny that he is unhappy, but nevertheless he is guilty.

---

[4] See §§7.1-7.2.
[5] See §7.5.
[6] All of the following sentences would be perfectly correct without the **ne**.
[7] See §12.9.
[8] Note that these constructions and those in the following paragraph are accompanied by a subordinate clause in the subjunctive.

Je ne doute pas qu'on (ne) puisse arriver un jour sur la planète Mars.	*I don't doubt that someday we'll be able to land on the planet Mars.*

5. *In clauses forming the second part of a comparison.*

Cet homme est plus riche que vous (ne) pensez.	*That man is wealthier than you think.*
Ce travail est moins difficile qu'on (ne) croit généralement.	*This work is less difficult than people usually think.*

E.   THE VERB DEVOIR

The verb *devoir* can have the following meanings:

1. *To owe.*

Je lui dois dix francs.	*I owe him ten francs.*
Vous lui devez de l'argent.	*You owe him (her) money.*
Nous lui devons le respect.	*We owe him (her) respect.*

2. *Must, have to, be obliged, should, ought to.*[9]

Un officier doit être loyal.	*An officer must be loyal.*
Nous devrons lire ce livre.	*We'll have to read this book.*
Vous devriez[10] accepter.	*You should accept.*

In a negative sentence, **devoir** indicates an absolute prohibition:

On ne doit pas tuer.	*We must not kill.*

Usually the expression **ne pas être obligé** indicates that an action is not absolutely necessary:

Vous n'êtes pas obligé d'aller à la cérémonie.	*You need not (You don't have to) go to the ceremony.*

3. *To be likely, to be supposed to, must (probability).*

Il n'est pas venu ce matin; il doit être malade.	*He didn't come this morning; he must be (he is probably) sick.*
Je ne l'ai pas vu; il a dû partir de bonne heure.	*I haven't seen him; he must have left early.*[11]

---

[9] Note the noun **le devoir:** *duty;* (pl.) *homework (of a student).*

[10] Concerning the present conditional of **devoir,** see below.

[11] In many cases the context indicates whether **devoir** expresses an obligation or a probability. In this sentence, for instance, **il a dû partir de bonne heure** could mean: *he has been obliged to (he had to) leave early.*

1. *In the present conditional,* **devoir** *indicates advice.*

Vous devriez étudier cette leçon.　　　*You should study this lesson.*

2. *In the past conditional, it indicates that the action never materialized.*[12]

J'aurais dû écrire cette lettre mais　　*I should have written this letter but*
j'ai oublié.　　　　　　　　　　　　*I forgot.*

3. *In the imperfect, it expresses either a repeated obligation or an action that never materialized.*[13]

Quand j'avais dix ans je devais　　*When I was ten years old I had to*
aller à l'école chaque jour.　　　　*go to school every day.*
Le Président Kennedy devait faire　*President Kennedy was to give a*
un discours à Dallas le 22 novem-　*speech in Dallas on November*
bre 1963.　　　　　　　　　　　　*22, 1963.*

4. *In the past participle,* **dû(e)** *means due, owed, because of.*

L'argent est dû.　　　　　　　　　*The money is due.*
L'accident a été dû à la pluie.　　*The accident was caused by the rain.*
Dû à la tempête, l'avion est en re-　*Due to the storm, the plane is late.*
tard.

§14.8

F.　MÊME

The meaning of **même** depends on its position in the sentence.

1. **Même** means *same* in the following instances (see §14.1):

article
demonstrative adj. } + **même (mêmes)** + noun
possessive adj.

2. When it follows the noun it means *the very, the specific, the essence of.*

Voici le livre même que je cher-　*Here is the very book that I was*
chais.　　　　　　　　　　　　　*looking for.*
Cette femme est la bonté même.　*That woman is kindness itself.*

---

[12] This is consistent with the normal meaning of the past conditional. See §11.13.
[13] This is peculiar to the verb **devoir**.

3. When it stands between two nouns, two adjectives, or two clauses it means *even*.

Tout le monde[14] **travaillait: les hommes, les femmes et même les enfants.**	*Everybody was working: the men, the women, and even the children.*
Cet étudiant est intelligent; il est même remarquable.	*This student is intelligent; he is even remarkable.*

4. It means *self* when followed by a disjunctive pronoun:

moi-même	*myself*	**nous-même(s)**	*ourself, -ves*
toi-même	*yourself*	**vous-même(s)**	*yourself, -ves*
lui-même	*himself*	**eux-mêmes**	*themselves*
elle-même	*herself*	**elles-mêmes**	*themselves*
soi-même	*oneself* [15]		

Il a construit sa maison lui-même.	*He built his house himself.*

5. The idiom **de même que** means *likewise, as . . . so.*

§14.9   G.   QUEL, QUELLE, QUELS, QUELLES

1. In interrogative sentences: *what, which* (see §4.12).

Quel journal lisez-vous?	*Which newspaper do you read (are you reading)?*
Quelle est la solution?	*What is the solution?*

2. In exclamatory sentences: *what a.*

Quelle erreur!	*What a mistake!*
Quelle surprise!	*What a surprise!*

3. Followed by **que** plus a verb in the subjunctive: *whatever* (see §12.12).

Quelles que soient les circonstances, je ferai mon devoir.	*Whatever the circumstances (may be), I will do my duty.*

---

[14] **Le monde:** *the world;* **tout le monde:** *everybody;* **le monde entier:** *the whole world.*
[15] This is the impersonal form.

H. QUELQUE, QUELQUES

1. When followed by an adjective or adverb plus **que** plus a verb in the subjunctive: *no matter how* (see §12.12).

Quelque brillant que vous soyez, vous devez néanmoins étudier vos leçons.	*No matter how brilliant you may be, you still have to study your lessons.*

2. When followed by a number: *about, some.*

Cette ville a quelque deux mille habitants.	*This town has about two thousand inhabitants.*

3. When followed by a noun: *some, any, a few.*

Il a quelques amis.	*He has a few friends.*
Il a parlé quelques minutes.	*He spoke for a few minutes.*
Avez-vous quelqu'ami qui puisse vous aider?	*Do you have some friend who can help you?*

When followed by a noun plus **que** plus a verb in the subjunctive, see §12.12.

Quelque is also found in several very common compound forms: **quelqu'un(e), quelques-un(e)s:** *someone, anyone,* (pl.) *some;* **quelque chose:** *something, anything;* **quelquefois:** *sometimes;* **quelque peu:** *somewhat.*

Quelqu'un vous attend.	*Somebody is waiting for you.*
Quelque chose de nouveau.	*Something new.*
Il vient quelquefois.	*He comes sometimes.*
Quelques-uns de nos amis.	*Some of our friends.*

I. TOUT, TOUTE, TOUS, TOUTES

The exact meaning of **tout** can be determined from its position in the sentence:

1. *All, the whole, the entire.*

$$\begin{matrix} \textbf{tout} \\ \textbf{toute} \end{matrix} + \left\{ \begin{matrix} \text{definite article} \\ \text{demonstrative adj.} \\ \text{possessive adj.} \end{matrix} \right\} + \text{singular noun}$$

129

toute la famille	*the whole family*
toute la surface	*the whole surface*
tout le livre	*the entire book*
tout le temps	*all the time*

2. *All, every.*

$$\begin{matrix} \textbf{tous} \\ \textbf{toutes} \end{matrix} + \left\{ \begin{matrix} \text{definite article} \\ \text{demonstrative adj.} \\ \text{possessive adj.} \end{matrix} \right\} + \text{plural noun}$$

tous les livres	*all the books*
toutes les règles	*all the rules*
tous les ans	*every year*
tous les cas	*all the cases, every single case*

3. *Any, any one, every.*

$$\begin{matrix} \textbf{tout} \\ \textbf{toute} \end{matrix} \right\} + \text{noun (without article)}$$

Tout enfant a besoin d'affection.	*Any (every) child needs affection.*
Toute désobéissance sera punie.	*Any disobedience will be punished.*

4. *Everything* (as the subject or object of a verb in the singular).

Tout n'est pas perdu.	*Everything is not lost.*
Il remarque tout.	*He notices everything.*
Il pense à tout.	*He thinks of everything.*

5. *All, all of them* (as the subject or object of a verb in the plural).

Tous sont partis.	*All of them left.*
Lisez ces lettres; lisez-les toutes.	*Read these letters; read them all.*

6. *Totally, completely, quite, all.*

$$\textbf{tout, toute} + \left\{ \begin{matrix} \text{adjective} \\ \text{present participle} \\ \text{past participle} \\ \text{preposition} \end{matrix} \right.$$

L'arbre était tout blanc.	*The tree was completely white.*
Il était tout étonné.	*He was quite surprised.*
Tout fumant.	*Steaming, covered with smoke.*
Tout près.	*Close by.*
Tout contre.	*Right against.*

7. **Le tout:** *the whole, the totality, the bulk.*

Il a acheté le tout pour dix francs.	*He bought the whole lot for ten francs.*
L'éducation doit former un tout.	*Education must form a whole.*

8. Idiomatic expressions:

tout à coup	*suddenly*
tout à fait	*completely*
tout à l'heure	*a little while ago, in a few minutes*[16]
tout de suite	*right away*[16]
tout en	*while*[17]
tout le monde	*everybody*[18]

---

[16] See §10.13.
[17] See §13.11.
[18] See note 14.

⊞ APPENDIX A ⊡

REGULAR VERBS

FIRST GROUP: MARCHER

INDICATIVE

PRESENT		PAST (PASSÉ COMPOSÉ)
je march	e	j'ai marché
tu march	es	tu as marché
il march	e	il a marché
nous march	ons	nous avons marché
vous march	ez	vous avez marché
ils march	ent	ils ont marché

IMPERFECT		PAST PERFECT
je march	ais	j'avais marché
tu march	ais	tu avais marché
il march	ait	il avait marché
nous march	ions	nous avions marché
vous march	iez	vous aviez marché
ils march	aient	ils avaient marché

PAST DEFINITE		PAST ANTERIOR
je march	ai	j'eus marché
tu march	as	tu eus marché
il march	a	il eut marché
nous march	âmes	nous eûmes marché
vous march	âtes	vous eûtes marché
ils march	èrent	ils eurent marché

	FUTURE		FUTURE PERFECT

je marcher	ai	j'aurai marché
tu marcher	as	tu auras marché
il marcher	a	il aura marché
nous marcher	ons	nous aurons marché
vous marcher	ez	vous aurez marché
ils marcher	ont	ils auront marché

CONDITIONAL

PRESENT | PAST

je marcher	ais	j'aurais marché
tu marcher	ais	tu aurais marché
il marcher	ait	il aurait marché
nous marcher	ions	nous aurions marché
vous marcher	iez	vous auriez marché
ils marcher	aient	ils auraient marché

IMPERATIVE

march	e
march	ons
march	ez

SUBJUNCTIVE

PRESENT | PAST

que je march	e	que j'aie marché
que tu march	es	que tu aies marché
qu'il march	e	qu'il ait marché
que nous march	ions	que nous ayons marché
que vous march	iez	que vous ayez marché
qu'ils march	ent	qu'ils aient marché

IMPERFECT

que je march	asse
que tu march	asses
qu'il march	ât
que nous march	assions
que vous march	assiez
qu'ils march	assent

PARTICIPLES

PRESENT	PAST
march $\boxed{\text{ant}}$	march $\boxed{\text{é}}$

SECOND GROUP: FINIR

INDICATIVE

PRESENT	PAST (PASSÉ COMPOSÉ)
je fin $\boxed{\begin{array}{l}\text{is}\\\text{is}\\\text{it}\\\text{issons}\\\text{issez}\\\text{issent}\end{array}}$	j'ai fini
tu fin	tu as fini
il fin	il a fini
nous fin	nous avons fini
vous fin	vous avez fini
ils fin	ils ont fini

IMPERFECT	PAST PERFECT
je fin $\boxed{\begin{array}{l}\text{issais}\\\text{issais}\\\text{issait}\\\text{issions}\\\text{issiez}\\\text{issaient}\end{array}}$	j'avais fini
tu fin	tu avais fini
il fin	il avait fini
nous fin	nous avions fini
vous fin	vous aviez fini
ils fin	ils avaient fini

PAST DEFINITE	PAST ANTERIOR
je fin $\boxed{\begin{array}{l}\text{is}\\\text{is}\\\text{it}\\\text{îmes}\\\text{îtes}\\\text{irent}\end{array}}$	j'eus fini
tu fin	tu eus fini
il fin	il eut fini
nous fin	nous eûmes fini
vous fin	vous eûtes fini
ils fin	ils eurent fini

FUTURE	FUTURE PERFECT
je finir $\boxed{\begin{array}{l}\text{ai}\\\text{as}\\\text{a}\\\text{ons}\\\text{ez}\\\text{ont}\end{array}}$	j'aurai fini
tu finir	tu auras fini
il finir	il aura fini
nous finir	nous aurons fini
vous finir	vous aurez fini
ils finir	ils auront fini

CONDITIONAL

<table>
<tr><td colspan="2" align="center">PRESENT</td><td align="center">PAST</td></tr>
<tr><td>je finir</td><td>ais</td><td>j'aurais fini</td></tr>
<tr><td>tu finir</td><td>ais</td><td>tu aurais fini</td></tr>
<tr><td>il finir</td><td>ait</td><td>il aurait fini</td></tr>
<tr><td>nous finir</td><td>ions</td><td>nous aurions fini</td></tr>
<tr><td>vous finir</td><td>iez</td><td>vous auriez fini</td></tr>
<tr><td>ils finir</td><td>aient</td><td>ils auraient fini</td></tr>
</table>

IMPERATIVE

fin | is
fin | issons
fin | issez

SUBJUNCTIVE

<table>
<tr><td colspan="2" align="center">PRESENT</td><td align="center">PAST</td></tr>
<tr><td>que je fin</td><td>isse</td><td>que j'aie fini</td></tr>
<tr><td>que tu fin</td><td>isses</td><td>que tu aies fini</td></tr>
<tr><td>qu'il fin</td><td>isse</td><td>qu'il ait fini</td></tr>
<tr><td>que nous fin</td><td>issions</td><td>que nous ayons fini</td></tr>
<tr><td>que vous fin</td><td>issiez</td><td>que vous ayez fini</td></tr>
<tr><td>qu'ils fin</td><td>issent</td><td>qu'ils aient fini</td></tr>
</table>

IMPERFECT

que je fin | isse
que tu fin | isses
qu'il fin | ît
que nous fin | issions
que vous fin | issiez
qu'ils fin | issent

PARTICIPLES

PRESENT   PAST

fin | issant   fin | i

Third Group: Vendre

INDICATIVE

PRESENT		PAST (PASSÉ COMPOSÉ)
je vend	s	j'ai vendu
tu vend	s	tu as vendu
il vend		il a vendu
nous vend	ons	nous avons vendu
vous vend	ez	vous avez vendu
ils vend	ent	ils ont vendu

IMPERFECT		PAST PERFECT
je vend	ais	j'avais vendu
tu vend	ais	tu avais vendu
il vend	ait	il avait vendu
nous vend	ions	nous avions vendu
vous vend	iez	vous aviez vendu
ils vend	aient	ils avaient vendu

PAST DEFINITE		PAST ANTERIOR
je vend	is	j'eus vendu
tu vend	is	tu eus vendu
il vend	it	il eut vendu
nous vend	îmes	nous eûmes vendu
vous vend	îtes	vous eûtes vendu
ils vend	irent	ils eurent vendu

FUTURE		FUTURE PERFECT
je vendr	ai	j'aurai vendu
tu vendr	as	tu auras vendu
il vendr	a	il aura vendu
nous vendr	ons	nous aurons vendu
vous vendr	ez	vous aurez vendu
ils vendr	ont	ils auront vendu

CONDITIONAL

PRESENT		PAST
je vendr	ais	j'aurais vendu
tu vendr	ais	tu aurais vendu
il vendr	ait	il aurait vendu
nous vendr	ions	nous aurions vendu
vous vendr	iez	vous auriez vendu
ils vendr	aient	ils auraient vendu

IMPERATIVE

vend	s
vend	ons
vend	ez

SUBJUNCTIVE

PRESENT

que je vend	e
que tu vend	es
qu'il vend	e
que nous vend	ions
que vous vend	iez
qu'ils vend	ent

PAST

que j'aie vendu
que tu aies vendu
qu'il ait vendu
que nous ayons vendu
que vous ayez vendu
qu'ils aient vendu

IMPERFECT

que je vend	isse
que tu vend	isses
qu'il vend	ît
que nous vend	issions
que vous vend	issiez
qu'ils vend	issent

PARTICIPLES

PRESENT

vend	ant

PAST

vend	u

138

⎸⎾ APPENDIX B ⏋

AUXILIARY VERBS

Être

INDICATIVE

PRESENT | PAST (PASSÉ COMPOSÉ)

je	suis	j'ai été
tu	es	tu as été
il	est	il a été
nous	sommes	nous avons été
vous	êtes	vous avez été
ils	sont	ils ont été

IMPERFECT | PAST PERFECT

j'	étais	j'avais été
tu	étais	tu avais été
il	était	il avait été
nous	étions	nous avions été
vous	étiez	vous aviez été
ils	étaient	ils avaient été

PAST DEFINITE | PAST ANTERIOR

je	fus	j'eus été
tu	fus	tu eus été
il	fut	il eut été
nous	fûmes	nous eûmes été
vous	fûtes	vous eûtes été
ils	furent	ils eurent été

	FUTURE	FUTURE PERFECT
je	serai	j'aurai été
tu	seras	tu auras été
il	sera	il aura été
nous	serons	nous aurons été
vous	serez	vous aurez été
ils	seront	ils auront été

CONDITIONAL

	PRESENT	PAST
je	serais	j'aurais été
tu	serais	tu aurais été
il	serait	il aurait été
nous	serions	nous aurions été
vous	seriez	vous auriez été
ils	seraient	ils auraient été

IMPERATIVE

sois
soyons
soyez

SUBJUNCTIVE

	PRESENT	PAST
que je	sois	qu j'aie été
que tu	sois	que tu aies été
qu'il	soit	qu'il ait été
que nous	soyons	que nous ayons été
que vous	soyez	que vous ayez été
qu'ils	soient	qu'ils aient été

IMPERFECT

que je	fusse
que tu	fusses
qu'il	fût
que nous	fussions
que vous	fussiez
qu'ils	fussient

PARTICIPLES

PRESENT	PAST
étant	été

Avoir

INDICATIVE

PRESENT

j'	ai
tu	as
il	a
nous	avons
vous	avez
ils	ont

PAST (PASSÉ COMPOSÉ)

j'ai eu
tu as eu
il a eu
nous avons eu
vous avez eu
ils ont eu

IMPERFECT

j'	avais
tu	avais
il	avait
nous	avions
vous	aviez
ils	avaient

PAST PERFECT

j'avais eu
tu avais eu
il avait eu
nous avions eu
vous aviez eu
ils avaient eu

PAST DEFINITE

j'	eus
tu	eus
il	eut
nous	eûmes
vous	eûtes
ils	eurent

PAST ANTERIOR

j'eus eu
tu eus eu
il eut eu
nous eûmes eu
vous eûtes eu
ils eurent eu

FUTURE

j'	aurai
tu	auras
il	aura
nous	aurons
vous	aurez
ils	auront

FUTURE PERFECT

j'aurai eu
tu auras eu
il aura eu
nous aurons eu
vous aurez eu
ils auront eu

CONDITIONAL

<table>
<tr><td align="center">PRESENT</td><td align="center">PAST</td></tr>
<tr><td>j' aurais</td><td>j'aurais eu</td></tr>
<tr><td>tu aurais</td><td>tu aurais eu</td></tr>
<tr><td>il aurait</td><td>il aurait eu</td></tr>
<tr><td>nous aurions</td><td>nous aurions eu</td></tr>
<tr><td>vous auriez</td><td>vous auriez eu</td></tr>
<tr><td>ils auraient</td><td>ils auraient eu</td></tr>
</table>

IMPERATIVE

aie
ayons
ayez

SUBJUNCTIVE

<table>
<tr><td align="center">PRESENT</td><td align="center">PAST</td></tr>
<tr><td>que j' aie</td><td>que j'aie eu</td></tr>
<tr><td>que tu aies</td><td>que tu aies eu</td></tr>
<tr><td>qu'il ait</td><td>qu'il ait eu</td></tr>
<tr><td>que nous ayons</td><td>que nous ayons eu</td></tr>
<tr><td>que vous ayez</td><td>que vous ayez eu</td></tr>
<tr><td>qu'ils aient</td><td>qu'ils aient eu</td></tr>
</table>

IMPERFECT

que j' eusse
que tu eusses
qu'il eût
que nous eussions
que vous eussiez
qu'ils eussent

PARTICIPLES

<table>
<tr><td align="center">PRESENT</td><td align="center">PAST</td></tr>
<tr><td>ayant</td><td>eu</td></tr>
</table>

ALLER.

INDICATIVE

<table>
<tr><td>PRESENT</td><td>PAST (PASSÉ COMPOSÉ)</td></tr>
<tr><td>je vais</td><td>je suis allé</td></tr>
<tr><td>tu vas</td><td>tu es allé</td></tr>
<tr><td>il va</td><td>il (elle) est allé(e)</td></tr>
<tr><td>nous allons</td><td>nous sommes allés</td></tr>
<tr><td>vous allez</td><td>vous êtes allés</td></tr>
<tr><td>ils vont</td><td>ils (elles) sont allé(e)s</td></tr>
</table>

<table>
<tr><td>IMPERFECT</td><td>PAST PERFECT</td></tr>
<tr><td>j' allais</td><td>j'étais allé</td></tr>
<tr><td>tu allais</td><td>tu étais allé</td></tr>
<tr><td>il allait</td><td>il (elle) était allé(e)</td></tr>
<tr><td>nous allions</td><td>nous étions allés</td></tr>
<tr><td>vous alliez</td><td>vous étiez allés</td></tr>
<tr><td>ils allaient</td><td>ils (elles) étaient allé(e)s</td></tr>
</table>

<table>
<tr><td>PAST DEFINITE</td><td>PAST ANTERIOR</td></tr>
<tr><td>j' allai</td><td>je fus allé</td></tr>
<tr><td>tu allas</td><td>tu fus allé</td></tr>
<tr><td>il alla</td><td>il (elle) fut allé(e)</td></tr>
<tr><td>nous allâmes</td><td>nous fûmes allés</td></tr>
<tr><td>vous allâtes</td><td>vous fûtes allés</td></tr>
<tr><td>ils allèrent</td><td>ils (elles) furent allé(e)s</td></tr>
</table>

<table>
<tr><td>FUTURE</td><td>FUTURE PERFECT</td></tr>
<tr><td>j' irai</td><td>je serai allé</td></tr>
<tr><td>tu iras</td><td>tu seras allé</td></tr>
<tr><td>il ira</td><td>il (elle) sera allé(e)</td></tr>
<tr><td>nous irons</td><td>nous serons allés</td></tr>
<tr><td>vous irez</td><td>vous serez allés</td></tr>
<tr><td>ils iront</td><td>ils (elles) seront allé(e)s</td></tr>
</table>

CONDITIONAL

<table>
<tr><td>PRESENT</td><td>PAST</td></tr>
<tr><td>j' irais</td><td>je serais allé</td></tr>
<tr><td>tu irais</td><td>tu serais allé</td></tr>
<tr><td>il irait</td><td>il (elle) serait allé(e)</td></tr>
<tr><td>nous irions</td><td>nous serions allés</td></tr>
<tr><td>vous iriez</td><td>vous seriez allés</td></tr>
<tr><td>ils iraient</td><td>ils (elles) seraient allé(e)s</td></tr>
</table>

IMPERATIVE

va
allons
allez

SUBJUNCTIVE

PRESENT

que j' aille
que tu ailles
qu'il aille
que nous allions
que vous alliez
qu'ils aillent

PAST

que je sois allé
que tu sois allé
qu'il (elle) soit allé(e)
que nous soyons allés
que vous soyez allés
qu'ils (elles) soient allé(e)s

IMPERFECT

que j' allasse
que tu allasses
qu'il allât
que nous allassions
que vous allassiez
qu'ils allassent

PARTICIPLE

PRESENT

allant

PAST

allé

⌦ APPENDIX C ⌫

THE FIVE PRINCIPAL PARTS
OF IRREGULAR VERBS*

In most cases, it is sufficient to know the five principal parts of an irregular verb, for the entire conjugation can usually be derived from them.

PRINCIPAL PARTS	DERIVED FORMS
infinitive	future tense present conditional (exceptions, see §10.4)
present participle	(1) imperfect (cf. the irregular verbs of §§8.2, 13.10) (2) certain forms of the present subjunctive (see §12.3) (3) most plural persons of the present indicative
past participle	all compound tenses
present indicative	imperative
past definite	. . .

INFINITIVE	PRESENT PARTICIPLE	PAST PARTICIPLE	PRESENT INDICATIVE	PAST DEFINITE
aller	allant	allé	vais	allai
apercevoir	apercevant	aperçu	aperçois	aperçus
apprendre	apprenant	appris	apprends	appris
boire	buvant	bu	bois	bus
comprendre	comprenant	compris	comprends	compris

---

* **Etre** and **avoir** excluded.

INFINITIVE	PRESENT PARTICIPLE	PAST PARTICIPLE	PRESENT INDICATIVE	PAST DEFINITE
conduire	conduisant	conduit	conduis	conduisis
connaître	connaissant	connu	connais	connus
craindre	craignant	craint	crains	craignis
croire	croyant	cru	crois	crus
devoir	devant	dû	dois	dus
dire	disant	dit	dis	dis
dormir	dormant	dormi	dors	dormis
écrire	écrivant	écrit	écris	écrivis
faire	faisant	fait	fais	fis
lire	lisant	lu	lis	lus
mettre	mettant	mis	mets	mis
mourir	mourant	mort	meurs	mourus
naître	naissant	né	nais	naquis
ouvrir	ouvrant	ouvert	ouvre	ouvris
partir	partant	parti	pars	partis
plaindre	plaignant	plaint	plains	plaignis
pouvoir	pouvant	pu	peux	pus
prendre	prenant	pris	prends	pris
produire	produisant	produit	produis	produisis
recevoir	recevant	reçu	reçois	reçus
savoir	sachant	su	sais	sus
sentir	sentant	senti	sens	sentis
servir	servant	servi	sers	servis
sortir	sortant	sorti	sors	sortis
suffire	suffisant	suffi	suffis	suffis
tenir	tenant	tenu	tiens	tins
venir	venant	venu	viens	vins
vivre	vivant	vécu	vis	vécus
voir	voyant	vu	vois	vis
vouloir	voulant	voulu	veux	voulus

ᛸ APPENDIX D ᛸ

FRENCH TENSES
AND THEIR ENGLISH EQUIVALENTS

TENSE	FRENCH	ENGLISH	WHERE DISCUSSED
PRESENT INDICATIVE	il travaille	*he works*	§§3.3-3.4
		he is working	§3.3
		he does work	§3.3
		he has been working	§§3.5, 9.10
		he is about to work	§3.6
		he worked	§3.7
PASSÉ COMPOSÉ	il a travaillé	*he has worked*	§3.12
		he worked	§3.12
IMPERFECT	il travaillait	*he was working*	§§8.4, 8.6
		he used to work	§8.5
		he had been working	§9.11
PAST DEFINITE	il travailla	*he worked*	§8.9
PAST PERFECT	il avait travaillé	*he had worked*	§§9.3, 9.4
		he worked	§9.3
PAST ANTERIOR	il eut travaillé	*he had worked*	§9.6
		he worked	§9.6
FUTURE	il travaillera	*he will work*	§10.5
		(when) he works	§10.6
		he will have worked	§9.12
FUTURE PERFECT	il aura travaillé	*he will have worked*	§10.10
		(when) he has worked	§10.11
		he has probably worked	§10.12
PRESENT CONDITIONAL	il travaillerait	*he would work*	§§11.5, 11.7-11.9
		he might work	§11.6

PAST CONDITIONAL	il aurait travaillé	*he would have worked* *he may have worked*	§§11.13-11.14 §11.12
IMPERATIVE	travaille(z, -ons)	*work! (let us work!)*	§3.14
PRESENT SUBJUNCTIVE	qu'il travaille	*that he works* *that he is working* *that he will work* *him to work* *though he works* *that he may work* *that he must work* *let him work* *that he worked*	§§12.6, 12.9-12.10 §§12.6, 12.9-12.10 §12.6 §12.7 §12.12 §12.12 §12.8 §12.13 §12.18
PAST SUBJUNCTIVE	qu'il ait travaillé	*that he has worked* *that he had worked* *him to have worked*	§12.16 §12.16 §12.17
IMPERFECT SUBJUNCTIVE	qu'il travaillât	*that he would work* *that he might work* *that he may work*	§12.18 §12.18 §12.18
PAST PERFECT SUBJUNCTIVE	qu'il eut travaillé	*that he had worked*	§12.19
INFINITIVE	travailler	*to work, (him) to work* *working*	§13.1-13.7 §13.8
PAST PARTICIPLE	travaillé	*worked*	§3.10
PRESENT PARTICIPLE	travaillant	*working*	§13.11-13.13

☐ APPENDIX E ☐

STEMS OF IRREGULAR VERBS*

Irregular verb forms, because they often differ so radically from the spelling of the infinitive, are difficult to look up in a dictionary. The following alphabetical listing of stems with their corresponding infinitives should therefore be helpful.

STEM	INFINITIVE	STEM	INFINITIVE
absolv-	absoudre	aperç-	apercevoir
absou-	absoudre	aperçoiv-	apercevoir
absten-	abstenir	apparaiss-	apparaître
abstien-	abstenir	apparten-	appartenir
abstiendr-	abstenir	appartien-	appartenir
abstienn-	abstenir	appartiendr-	appartenir
abstin-	abstenir	appartienn-	appartenir
accroi-	accroître	appartin-	appartenir
accroiss-	accroître	apparu-	apparaître
accru-	accroître	appren-	apprendre
acquerr-	acquérir	appri-	apprendre
acqui-	acquérir	astreign-	astreindre
acquièr-	acquérir	astreint-	astreindre
adjoign-	adjoindre	atteign-	atteindre
adjoin-	adjoindre	atteint-	atteindre
adjoint-	adjoindre	asseoi-	asseoir
adven-	advenir	assey-	asseoir
advien-	advenir	assi-	asseoir
adviendr-	advenir	assied-	asseoir
advienn-	advenir	assiér-	asseoir
advin-	advenir	assoi-	asseoir
aill-	aller	assoir-	asseoir
all-	aller	assoy-	asseoir

* **Etre** and **avoir** excluded.

STEM	INFINITIVE	STEM	INFINITIVE
bat-	battre	cous-	coudre
batt-	battre	cousi-	coudre
battu-	battre	cousu-	coudre
boi-	boire	craign-	craindre
boiv-	boire	crain-	craindre
bou-	bouillir	craint-	craindre
bouill-	bouillir	croi-	croire
bu-	boire	croî-	croître
buv-	boire	croiss-	croître
ceign-	ceindre	croy-	croire
ceint-	ceindre	cru-	croire
circonscri-	circonscrire	crû-	croître
circonscriv-	circonscrire	cui-	cuire
clo-	clore	cuis-	cuire
clor-	clore	cuit-	cuire
compar-	comparaître	déç-	décevoir
comparaiss-	comparaître	déchu-	déchoir
comparu-	comparaître	déçoiv-	décevoir
complais-	complaire	décri-	décrire
complu-	complaire	décriv-	décrire
compren-	comprendre	décroi-	décroître
compri-	comprendre	décroiss-	décroître
conç-	concevoir	décru-	décroître
conclu-	conclure	défai-	défaire
conçoiv-	concevoir	défais-	défaire
condui-	conduire	défass-	défaire
conduis-	conduire	défer-	défaire
conduit-	conduire	défi-	défaire
confit-	confire	déplais-	déplaire
connai-	connaître	déplu-	déplaire
connaiss-	connaître	dépourvoy-	dépourvoir
connu-	connaître	dépourvu-	dépourvoir
construi-	construire	détrui-	détruire
construis-	construire	détruis-	détruire
construit-	construire	détruit-	détruire
conten-	contenir	dev-	devoir
contien-	contenir	di-	dire
contiendr-	contenir	dis-	dire
contienn-	contenir	disjoign-	disjoindre
contin-	contenir	disjoin-	disjoindre
convainc-	convaincre	disjoint-	disjoindre
convaincu-	convaincre	dispar-	disparaître
convainqu-	convaincre	disparaiss-	disparaître
conven-	convenir	disparu-	disparaître
convien-	convenir	dissolv-	dissoudre
conviendr-	convenir	dissou-	dissoudre
convienn-	convenir	distrait-	distraire
convin-	convenir	distray-	distraire
coud-	coudre	dit-	dire
cour-	courir	doi-	devoir
courr-	courir	doiv-	devoir

dor-	dormir	faill-	faillir
dorm-	dormir	fais-	faire
dû-	devoir	fait-	faire
échu-	échoir	fall-	falloir
écri-	écrire	fass-	faire
écrit-	écrire	fau-	falloir
écriv-	écrire	faud-	falloir
éli-	élire	feign-	feindre
élis-	élire	feint-	feindre
élu-	élire	fer-	faire
émet-	émettre	fi-	faire
émeuv-	émouvoir	fri-	frire
émi-	émettre	frit-	frire
empregn-	empreindre	fui-	fuir
empreint-	empreindre	fuy-	fuir
ému-	émouvoir	indui-	induire
enclo-	enclore	induis-	induire
enduis-	enduire	induit-	induire
enduit-	enduire	inscri-	inscrire
enfreign-	enfreindre	inscriv-	inscrire
enfreint-	enfreindre	instrui-	instruire
enfui-	enfuir	instruit-	instruire
enfuy-	enfuir	interdis-	interdire
enjoign-	enjoindre	interdit-	interdire
enjoin-	enjoindre	introdui-	introduire
enquer-	enquérir	introduis-	introduire
enquerr-	enquérir	introduit-	introduire
enqui-	enquérir	ir-	aller
enquier-	enquérir	joign-	joindre
ensuit-	ensuivre	join-	joindre
ensuiv-	ensuivre	joint-	joindre
entretien-	entretenir	li-	lire
entretiendr-	entretenir	lir-	lire
entretienn-	entretenir	lis-	lire
entretin-	entretenir	lu-	lire
entrev-	entrevoir	lui-	luire
entreverr-	entrevoir	luis-	luire
entrevoy-	entrevoir	mainten-	maintenir
entrevu-	entrevoir	maintien-	maintenir
équival-	équivaloir	maintiendr-	maintenir
équivau-	équivaloir	maintienn-	maintenir
équivaudr-	équivaloir	maintin-	maintenir
éteign-	éteindre	maudir-	maudire
éteint-	éteindre	maudis-	maudire
étreign-	étreindre	maudit-	maudire
étreint-	étreindre	méconnai-	méconnaître
exclu-	exclure	méconnaiss-	méconnaître
extrait-	extraire	méconnu-	méconnaître
extray-	extraire	médis-	médire
fai-	faire	médit-	médire
faill-	falloir	men-	mentir

STEM	INFINITIVE		STEM	INFINITIVE
méprenn-	méprendre		pren-	prendre
méprenn-	méprendre		prend-	prendre
mépri-	méprendre		prenn-	prendre
met-	mettre		prescrit-	prescrire
meu-	mouvoir		prescriv-	prescrire
meur-	mourir		pri-	prendre
meuv-	mouvoir		promet-	promettre
mi-	mettre		promi-	promettre
mis-	mettre		promis-	promettre
mort-	mourir		promu-	promouvoir
moud-	moudre		proven-	provenir
moulu-	moudre		provenu-	provenir
mourr-	mourir		provien-	provenir
mû-	mouvoir		proviendr-	provenir
nai-	naître		provin-	provenir
naiss-	naître		pu-	pouvoir
naqui-	naître		pui-	pouvoir
né-	naître		recev-	recevoir
nui-	nuire		reçoi-	recevoir
nuis-	nuire		reçu-	recevoir
obten-	obtenir		renai-	renaître
obtien-	obtenir		renaiss-	renaître
obtiendr-	obtenir		renaqui-	renaître
obtin-	obtenir		rend-	rendre
obtenu-	obtenir		rendu-	rendre
oint-	oindre		repu-	repaître
paiss-	paître		résolu-	résoudre
parai-	paraître		résolv-	résoudre
paraiss-	paraître		résou-	résoudre
paru-	paraître		restreign-	restreindre
peign-	peindre		restrein-	restreindre
pein-	peindre		restreint-	restreindre
peint-	peindre		reverr-	revoir
percev-	percevoir		revi-	revoir
percevr-	percevoir		revi-	revivre
perçoi-	percevoir		revoi-	revoir
perçoiv-	percevoir		revoy-	revoir
perçu-	percevoir		revu-	revoir
peu-	pouvoir		ri-	rire
plai-	plaire		romp-	rompre
plais-	plaire		rompu-	rompre
pleu-	pleuvoir		sach-	savoir
plu-	pleuvoir		sai-	savoir
plu-	plaire		sau-	savoir
pour-	pouvoir		sav-	savoir
pourvoi-	pourvoir		sédui-	séduire
pourvoy-	pourvoir		séduis-	séduire
pourvu-	pourvoir		séduit-	séduire
pouv-	pouvoir		ser-	servir
prédis-	prédire		sey-	seoir
prédit-	prédire		sied-	seoir

STEM	INFINITIVE	STEM	INFINITIVE
souff-	souffrir	transcriv-	transcrire
soumet-	soumettre	transmet-	transmettre
soumis-	soumettre	transmi-	transmettre
souscri-	souscrire	tu-	taire
souscriv-	souscrire	va-	aller
souten-	soutenir	vai-	aller
soutien-	soutenir	vaill-	valoir
soutiendr-	soutenir	vainc-	vaincre
soutienn-	soutenir	vaincu-	vaincre
soutin-	soutenir	vainqu-	vaincre
su-	savoir	val-	valoir
subven-	subvenir	valu-	valoir
subvien-	subvenir	vau-	valoir
subviendr-	subvenir	vaudr-	valoir
subvienn-	subvenir	vécu-	vivre
subvin-	subvenir	ven-	venir
suffis-	suffire	verr-	voir
sui-	suivre	veu-	vouloir
surpren-	surprendre	veuill-	vouloir
surpri-	surprendre	vi-	vivre
sursi-	surseoir	vi-	voir
tais-	taire	vien-	venir
teign-	teindre	viendr-	venir
teint-	teindre	vienn-	venir
ten-	tenir	vin-	venir
tien-	tenir	viv-	vivre
tiendr-	tenir	voi-	voir
tienn-	tenir	voudr-	vouloir
tin-	tenir	voul-	vouloir
tradui-	traduire	voy-	voir
traduis-	traduire	vu-	voir
transcri-	transcrire		

⌐ APPENDIX F ⌐

NUMERALS

CARDINAL NUMBERS

1	un, une	17	dix-sept	61	soixante et un
2	deux	18	dix-huit	62	soixante-deux, etc.
3	trois	19	dix-neuf	70	soixante-dix
4	quatre	20	vingt	71	soixante et onze
5	cinq	21	vingt et un	72	soixante-douze, etc.
6	six	22	vingt-deux, etc.	80	quatre-vingts
7	sept	30	trente	81	quatre-vingt-un
8	huit	31	trente et un	82	quatre-vingt-deux
9	neuf	32	trente-deux, etc.	90	quatre-vingt-dix
10	dix	40	quarante	91	quatre-vingt-onze
11	onze	41	quarante et un	92	quatre-vingt-douze, etc.
12	douze	42	quarante-deux, etc.	100	cent
13	treize	50	cinquante	101	cent un
14	quartorze	51	cinquante et un	102	cent deux, etc.
15	quinze	52	cinquante-deux, etc.	1000	mille
16	seize	60	soixante	1001	mille un, etc.

ORDINAL NUMBERS

Ordinal numbers are formed by adding **-ième** to the cardinal number. There is only one exception: **premier** (*first*).

1st	premier, première
2nd	deuxième *or* second (*m.*), seconde (*f.*)
3rd	troisième
4th	quatrième
10th	dixième

20th	vingtième
21st	vingt et unième
22nd	vingt-deuxième

FRACTIONS

½	demi (*adj.*); la moitié (*noun*)
¼	un quart
¾	trois quarts
⅓	un tiers
⅔	deux tiers

With other fractions, the denominator is an ordinal number as in English:

³⁄₁₀	trois dixièmes

⌜ INDEX ⌝